By the Voice of the Spirit

By the Voice of the Spirit

A Spiritual Critique for Ministers and Laity of all Religious Affiliations, and non believers

Alberta Anderson, RN, Ed.D

authorHOUSE®

AuthorHouse™
1663 Liberty Drive
Bloomington, IN 47403
www.authorhouse.com
Phone: 1-800-839-8640

First published by AuthorHouse   09/28/2011

ISBN: 978-1-4634-1060-5 (sc)
ISBN: 978-1-4634-1059-9 (hc)
ISBN: 978-1-4634-3854-8 (ebk)

Library of Congress Control Number: 2011908659

Printed in the United States of America

Any people depicted in stock imagery provided by Thinkstock are models, and such images are being used for illustrative purposes only.
Certain stock imagery © Thinkstock.

This book is printed on acid-free paper.

DEDICATION

I would like to dedicate this book to God, my most loving and generous Heavenly Father; and to Jesus, His Son, and my Brother, Majestic Conquering Lion of Judah, for loving me enough to die for me; and to the Holy Spirit, Who without His guidance, this book would not be possible.

I wish to honor the late Thomas and Mary Anderson, my parents, who gave me the love, guidance, structure, and discipline to set me on my physical and spiritual path. Although I sometimes strayed, I always knew where "home" (morals, ethics, values) was, and how to get back there. Thank you daddy and mama! I love you always!

To my daughter, E. Marie Brown, who is a wonderful daughter, best friend, mother, and confidant. Thank you for letting me cry on your shoulder when I needed to. Thank you for your insightful wisdom, far beyond your years. You are food for my soul! I love you so much!

To my son, Joseph Bolding, you *are* more than a conqueror. I love you so much!

To my grandsons, Mason and Tyler Brown, young men of God, who made me laugh despite any circumstance, and quoted back what I taught them, when I needed to hear it. You are dessert for my soul. I love you to the far ends of the universe and back!

To my granddaughters Alexa and Tory Bolding who are the delights of my heart and will grow up to be Proverbs 31 women. I love you from afar and back!

To my best friends, Bette Burgess, Trisha Ervin, my cousin, Carolyn Bolding, Tonecia McMillan, Sandra Howard, Barbara Collins, Angelina Langston, Dorothy Kelley, and Terry Murphy thank you for your loyal friendships, and for being my strong prayer partners, and having "church" with me whenever I needed it. I love you all!

To Pastor Alfred and Mrs. Beverly Craig, Sister Glorya, and Sister Libby, thank you for extending my search for the truth, setting me on my *deep* Spiritual path, and teaching me how to find the Father's loving and forgiving heart. Thank you for all the spiritual food.

To all, of many denominations, and are too numerous to mention, thank you for your very significant roles in my journey.

May the favor and blessings of the Lord be with all of you always! See you in Zion!!!

TABLE OF CONTENTS

*Liberty has been taken to capitalize all references to God, Jesus Christ, and the Holy Spirit in Scripture. Lower case letters are purposely used for all satanic organizations throughout the book.

EQUIPPED WITH THE WORD OF GOD

"Every tongue should confess that Jesus Christ is Lord."
(Philippians 2:11)

Being equipped with the Word of God is a process of continuous study, unceasing prayer, and a reverent desire to understand God's Nature, Spirit, commands and statutes, as well as His expectation of how His Gospel is to be spread. Because God holds us responsible for the souls of others, it is more than imperative that what we teach is scriptural, correct, true, and under the guidance of the Holy Spirit.

"But as touching brotherly love you need not that I write unto you: for ye yourselves are taught of God to love one another. And indeed ye do it toward all the brethren which are in Macedonia: but we beseech you, brethren, that ye increase more and more; and that ye study to be quiet, and to work your own business, and to work with your own hands, as we commanded you; that ye may walk honestly toward them that are without, that ye may have lack of nothing."
(2 Timothy 4: 9-12)

In order to accomplish this, we must understand the nature of God (to the extent that we can, with our finite minds) and develop a very personal relationship with Him. It is well to praise and worship God corporately, but each man must seek his own personal relationship with God in (reverent) fear and trembling. We must praise and worship Him individually as we develop a very personal relationship with Him. We must get to know God through His unchanging Word, understand His plan for mankind's salvation, and His methodology in seeing His plan to fruition. In addition to this, we must understand the nature of Jesus and strive to be like Him in kindness, long suffering, and great love for one another. We must also understand Jesus' role in God's plan—pre, and especially post crucifixion. Studying God's word in scripture by Holy Ghost power is key to acquiring, and understanding this knowledge, so that we may become equipped with Holy Ghost Power.

> "And He humbled thee, and suffered thee to hunger, and fed thee with manna, which ye knewest not, neither did thy fathers know; that He might make thee know that man doth not live by bread only, but by every word that proceedeth out of the mouth of the Lord doth man live."
> (Deuteronomy 8:3)

Many mainstream churches teach doctrines that are not of God, but doctrines of men. It is more than grandiose to believe that followers should follow one man's interpretation of the gospel, as if the Holy Spirit does not speak to anyone who seeks Him. This is a tactic to control the followers, and oppresses their zeal to seek God independently, personally, and outside of the pews of the church. It reeks of diabolical power, control, and illicit intent. More often than not, that one man is under the control of the evil one. What better tactic than to impose a religious system that impedes the followers from seeking the company of God personally, and outside of the church. The Holy Spirit will speak to anyone who seeks Him with a sincere heart. His knowledge and interpretation of the expectations of the Father represents a giant, whereas man's represents an ant!

"For false christs and false prophet shall rise, and shall shew signs and wonders, to seduce, if it were possible, even the elect."

(Mark 13: 22)

"A false witness shall perish . . . ."
(Proverbs 21: 28)

Most religious organizations *keep* Jesus on the cross of Calvary. Indeed He did go to the cross because of His love for the Father, and His love for us, but we need to evolve past this. Give thanks and praise for what He did for us on Calvary, then move on to worship, and understand the agenda of the Risen Christ. He is no longer in the role of the Lamb of God, Who takes away the sins of the world (crucifixion role); **He is now the risen Majestic, Conquering Lion of Judah (post crucifixion role),** Who will lead God's heavenly battle against the devil, his minions, and all manner of evil. We need to ask the Holy Spirit what *our* assignment is in preparation for this battle. This is done by praying the will of the Holy Spirit to the Majestic, Conquering Lion of Judah.

When we remain fixated on the cross, and cannot move to worship the Risen Christ, we impede our ability to become equipped Spiritually to prepare for battle. No doubt the devil delights in this type of Christian stagnation. The enemy cares not whether you go to church, sing, dance, pray before statues and pictures, or participate in church activities, as long as you are not receiving the truth, and are not actively participating in God's battle plan and His plan for mankind's salvation. Often church leaders plans are not in sync with the plan of God. They often loose sight of God's Divine plan with too many "church" activities, not necessarily of a spiritual nature, too many apologetic activities, and too much competition to see who can build the largest and most lavish church. All of this is not for God's glory, but is for man's vanity. It is not the size of the church or how lavish it is that matters, its whether or not the Holy Ghost enters there!

Does the Holy Ghost enter into your church!?

> "Teaching them to observe all things whatsoever I have commanded you: and, lo, I am with you always, even unto the end of the world."
> (Matthew 28:20)

When we continue to kneel and pray in front of crucifixes, and statues, fall asleep in church, and never commit to evangelism, and service to those in need, what good are we in spreading the news of the gospel, listening for the directives from the Holy Spirit, and becoming an active participant in God's plan? The enemy relishes this, it fits directly in *his* plan without any effort on his part. As leaders, we must wake up those that are asleep, both literally and figuratively, and encourage action on their parts, involving them in God's plan. **The churches need some shaking up!!! We must get back on task—soul saving, and building God's army on earth! Nothing else matters!**

> "And I saw the beast, and the kings of the earth, and their armies, gathered together to make war against Him that sat on the horse, and against His Army."
> (Revelations 19: 19)

> "For Thou hast girded me with strength to battle: them that rose up against me hast Thou subdued under me."
> (2 Samuel 22 :40)

Some priests, cardinals, pastors, bishops, ministers, rabbis, and their wives, are so puffed up with pride, ego, entitlement, and believe that they are so holy, and they are the only ones with whom God converses. They forget that they should be of service to others, not the opposite! They are no earthly good. They have stolen the Lord's glory, the followers riches, and practically have the followers worshipping them, and definitely have the followers serving them.

These modern day pharisees are more concerned with obtaining wealth through tithes and offerings, tape and book "ministries", and free service of "good works", all to their benefit. This is the epitome of wickedness. Again, the followers cannot find God because they cannot move past this exceedingly imperfect, charismatic, and often wicked man. God's men and women need to fix this immediately!!! Are you truly God's man or God's woman? To not fix a known ministerial mistake is an abominable sin before God. He holds His leaders to a much higher standard. To whom much is given, much is required!!!

> "Beloved, believe not every spirit, but try the spirits whether they are of God: because many false prophets are gone out into the world."
>
> (1 John 4:1)

This world and most world religions are under the dominion of the prince of darkness. The apostle John reminds us that the whole world languishes in the lap of the evil one. Never forget the power of the enemy, and never underestimate him. Demons keep track of details—there is a reason the Bible calls them "familiar spirits." The world of the occult offers mystery and power in thousands of different forms, but whether it is tarot cards, the black mass, or the daily horoscope, it is the same force. (We must not deal with these things, however innocent they may appear; they are tools of the adversary, and will capture you into a web of increasing evil.) The apostle John warned the church to guard their hearts and keep themselves from idols (1 John 5:21). An idol is a representation of a demon; a dangerous deception some may fall into if not prepared. The word keep is from the Greek word phulasso meaning "be on guard." Children be on guard. Guard against the demons by keeping away from idols, recognizing the place you have in Jesus Christ, and by putting on the whole armor of

God. "Put on the whole armour of God, that you may be able to stand against the wiles of the devil. For we do not wrestle against flesh and blood, but against principalities, against powers, against the rulers of the darkness of this age, against spiritual wickedness in the heavenly places." (Eph. 6: 11, 12) Jesus knew the difficulty of this struggle, and He prayed for the church. "I do not pray that you should take them out of the world, but that you should keep them from the evil one: (John 17:15). God has placed His Church in this world for a purpose, and that purpose is to resist the forces of darkness through the power of the Lord Jesus Christ.[1] The gospel of Jesus Christ is a way of life, and the only way to eternal life.

"Ye must press forward with a steadfastness in Christ, having a perfect brightness of hope, and a love of God and of all men. Wherefore, if ye shall press forward, feasting upon the Word of Christ, and endure to the end, behold, thus saith the Father: Ye shall have eternal life."

(2 Nephi 31: 20) (The Book of Mormon)

Preaching and teaching should be looked upon as an honor and privilege to serve God in the capacity of leading His lost sheep into, or back into the fold; imparting Revelation Knowledge in a manner that is easily understood, and lovingly and patiently provided, and providing whatever service is required. Service should be approached patiently, tirelessly, reverently, and lovingly. We should never make the congregations feel "less than," because we are the "grand poobahs" of the churches. Because we are the leaders, we must be in service to them. **It is being in service to God when we serve others,** one of the highest honors to be had. It requires being in tuned to the Holy Spirit at all times,

---

[1]   Martin, Walter, The Kingdom of the Occult, (1989), pg. 552

Who will reveal the needs of the recipient, and issues to be explored. Jesus said when you've done it for the least of my little ones, you've done it unto me. What a privilege to be of service to Jesus, the Majestic Conquering Lion of Judah!

> "Woe unto him that striveth with his Maker! . . . ."
> (Isaiah 45:9)

The most important thing in the spiritual life, is to ask for the gifts and fruits of the Holy Spirit Who addresses all of our needs (also in preaching, teaching and counseling). We can ask the Spirit for discernment, to extend our vision, for health, and most important we can ask the Holy Spirit how to pray to Him. (The Holy Spirit is a better instructor than any book or preacher). Pray to the Holy Spirit for enlightenment. (He will give us the information we seek) or lead us to where we should go for information and will choose the books we need to study. (He will Personally teach the Word in a manner easily understood and easily retained). Passages from the Bible become more vivid, meaningful and insightful when they are studied with His guidance. When we accept Him, we have the truth and cannot be deceived. The Spirit is truth and when we have that, we are released from our errors and bondages.[2]

> "And I will pray the Father, and He shall give you another
> Comforter, that He may abide with you forever; even the Spirit
> of Truth; Whom the world cannot receive, because it seeth
> Him not, neither knoweth Him; but ye know Him; for He
> dwelleth with you, and shall be in you."
> (John 14: 16,17)

---

[2] Brown, Michael H., <u>Prayer of the Warrior</u>, (1993), pg. 111

It is the Holy Spirit Who lifts our (spiritual) blindness and illuminates (Revelation knowledge). "You shall know the truth," thus do we see the importance of heartfelt prayer. Open your hearts to God like spring flowers which crave for the sun. When you pray, you are much more beautiful like flowers which after the snow, show all their beauty, and all their colors become indescribable.[3]

> "This then is the message which we have heard of Him, and declare unto you, that God is Light and in Him is no darkness at all. If we say that we have fellowship with Him, and walk in darkness, we lie, and do not the truth: But if we walk in the Light, as He is the Light, we have fellowship one with another, and the Blood of Jesus Christ His Son cleanseth us from all sin."
>
> (John 1:5-7)

Searching the scriptures under the guidance of the Holy Spirit is a daily constant. Genesis to Revelations should be studied with prayers for Divine Revelation, and the gift to impart this knowledge in its true and correct form under the guidance of the Holy Spirit. Scriptures must be studied and restudied again and again. With each new study,

new wisdom is imparted to strengthen our knowledge and to make us more improved teachers, preachers, counselors, and pastors. This ever increasing knowledge is imperative to meet the needs of those whom we teach. The Spirit is there to guide us in the appropriate subject matter and gives utterance to what is to be imparted to meet the needs of the recipient. ***He* is the Great Educator.**

---

[3]   Brown Michael H., <u>Prayer of the Warrior</u>, (1993) pg. 112

"Study to shew thyself approved unto God, a workman that needeth not to be ashamed, rightly dividing the Word of truth."

(2 Timothy 2:15)

The gift of discernment from the Holy Spirit is necessary to determine the needs, and sincerity of those who seek Revelation Knowledge. He is also our protection from deceiving spirits, and evil spirits who often manifest in human flesh. He protects us from those who are under the control of the evil one. We must be a conduit for the Holy Spirit in order to teach properly, and keep the individual engaged, and with a single desire to continue to build on the Knowledge of God. The guidance of the Spirit also protects us from becoming vain, puffed up, and intentionally or unintentionally stealing God's glory. He keeps us humble, modest, and respectful.

"But strong meat belongeth to them that are of full age, even those who by reason of use have their senses exercised to discern both good and evil"

(Hebrews 5:14)

Humanity all across the planet are in the midst of constant spiritual warfare. It is a political war in that it is a war waged in an unnatural and vanity ridden desire for power and control of all of God's creation. Both sides have a government in place—good and evil, with governing bodies, that follow the orders of their superiors. It is a cultural war, a clash of cultures of good and evil, right and wrong, and what is pure, and what is putrid. It's a war that has been brewing all of our lives, and since before the dawn of time. In every aspect of our lives, there has been an ongoing battle between the power of Divine Light and ominous darkness.

"For though we walk in the flesh, we do not war after the flesh:
For the weapons of our warfare are not carnal, but mighty
through God to the pulling down of strong holds; casting down
imaginations, and every high thing that exalteth itself against
the Knowledge of God, and bringing into captivity every
thought to the obedience of Christ; and having in a readiness
to revenge all disobedience, when your obedience is fulfilled."

(2 Corinthians 10: 3:6)

Don't be deceived, however, because the dark forces don't always manifest
as darkness. They often present as wolves in sheep's clothing, a very decisive
measure to camouflage evil intent. If you can identify your enemy it is
easier to protect yourself; if you cannot identify your enemy, you can be
so much more easily deceived. There are always two sides, which side are
you on? Are you on the Lord's side, and in His army, or not?

"For such are false apostles, deceitful workers, transforming
themselves into the Apostles of Christ. And no marvel; for
satan himself is transformed into an angel of light. Therefore
it is no great thing if his ministers also be transformed as the
ministers of righteousness; whose end shall be according to
their works."

(2 Corinthians 13-15)

On one side are those who have taken the path toward God, who think in
terms of the nature, heart, Spirit, and fragrance of Christ and their eternal
destination; on the other side, those who have fallen away from their faith
and wittingly or unwittingly support the workings of an actual supernatural
entity called the devil, the serpent, shaytan, shaitan, beelzebub, belial,
dragon, abaddon, amon, mastema, saitan, samael, shiva, son of perdition,
or satan. Right now it may seem that the dark is winning. Evil is rising as

never before. However, this is not the case. Good will always triumph over evil, because God is all powerful, and full of goodness!!

> "And they shall teach my people the difference between the Holy and profane, and cause them to discern between the unclean and the clean."
> (Ezekiel 44:23)

As evil spirals around the planet we see an increase in the crime rate, in the divorce rate, in the rate of abortions, in the number of teen pregnancies. We see it in Hollywood and the music industry that promote illicit sex, violence, and drug and alcohol abuse. We see it in child molestation by clergy, of most denominations. We see it in the Middle East, where fierce tribalism among Al Qaida, Hezbollah, Taliban, and other Muslims sects, has lead to thousands of rapes, tortures, mutilations and deaths. It is ongoing in the fires of the Middle East and parts of Africa, where the people are now fighting against centuries old oppression and control. We see it in the guns which have increased and now accompany pens and notebooks to school, we see it in the youths lack of respect for adults and authority figures, we see it in the very high numbers of those addicted to pharmaceutical narcotics (especially the elderly), the increase in teenage promiscuity, illegal drug abuse, child prostitution rings, homosexuality, and lesbianism. Most horridly, we see it in the numbers of boys molested by catholic priest for decades, perhaps centuries, and the vatican cover up. This double betrayal has increased the number of boys, who will grow into men with mental illness, and all types of personality disturbances, which will be passed down throughout the generations. A mentally unstable parent cannot raise a mentally stable child. This is a generational curse! How demonically inspired!!

(In the past, we've seen evil escalate in the mass suicides or mass killings by such as the Branch Davidians, Heavens Gate, Peoples Temple, Aum Supreme Truth as well as other so called religious groups defined as cults, and in mass murderers, rapists, and child molesters), we've see it on the face of a police officer in Olympia, Washington, who turned out to be a practicing satanist and was arrested for sexually abusing his own daughters. We've see it in New York, where Saint John the Divine Episcopalian Church, displayed a bronze sculpting called "Christa"—a nude woman on a cross—one Holy week, and had allowed a new age prophet to speak from the pulpit. We saw it in Colorado, where nuns prayed to the rising sun. We've see it in Louisiana where a famous evangelist was caught patronizing a prostitute.[4]

The most important thing in the spiritual life, is to ask for the gifts of the Holy Spirit Who addresses all of our needs. We can ask the Spirit for discernment and to extend our knowledge when all trust is gone. Where there is no trust, there can be no family, friendships, or communities. As a result there exists a breakdown of the family structure and the community structure. Family and friends are looked upon with suspicion. Friends now become "frienemies" (friends who are really enemies, rivals or not completely trusted). This leads to all types of estrangements from family, friends, and community.

We are all under this evil spiritual assault, unless we are covered by the Blood of Jesus, and the gifts of the Holy Spirit. This diabolical assault causes anxiety, depression, mood disorders, other mental illnesses, including suicide. There is an increase in the use of antidepressants, illicit drugs, pharmaceutical drugs, and alcohol. More people are self medicating in an effort to cope, in a seemingly hopeless world, however the problems remain once the drugs wear off and are compounded by the drug and alcohol abuse and dependence.

A culmination of these issues is causing division in our families, friendships, and community affiliations, as well as increased crime in our communities. It plagues us with confusion, doubts, paranoia, helplessness, and hopelessness. This war is waged on a supernatural stage, and in the deepest recesses of our beings, and minds; however, this is how it is manifested in the physical, and will overwhelm and over power us if we don't function under the guidance and power of the Holy Spirit.

---

4   Brown, Michael H., <u>Prayer of the Warrior</u>, (1993), pgs., 1, 2

These times are so evil, that this is not the time to think we can "go it alone," or think we "can handle" it. No! We cannot!! We are warring with very powerful supernatural entities that can snuff us out like a candle, if we are not under the protection of the Blood of Jesus and the guidance of Holy Spirit. In modern times, evil has increased dramatically, and the love of Christ has fallen away except for a very few of the faithful. This has been demonstrated by an increase in crime, a decrease in community involvement, corporate and government corruption, the failing economy and housing market; the bankers, lenders, and all on wall street, who have become exceedingly wealthier, on the pain, suffering, and tears of those on main street, even the government's clandestine involvement! High times on Wall Street, and very hard times on Main Street!

The governments of the world are all in bed together, kissing each other in the mouth, and plotting the total downfall of the entire world's economic system for wealth, and power—world domination, and to bring about the very wicked new world order, (a world of oppression, the new slavery, religious persecution, and political tyranny), this includes the one world religious system, the one world monetary system, the one world police state, and the one world government, described in the Book of Revelations. As a result, families, friendships and communities, townships, states, the entire country, and the entire world are quickly dissolving into nothingness, because of events the people don't quite understand, are powerless to control, and because of the *hidden agendas* of the extremely wealthy, wicked, and politically powerful.

> "For the mystery of iniquity doth already work: only he who now letteth will let, until he be taken out of the way. And then shall that wicked be revealed, whom the Lord shall consume with the Spirit of His mouth, and shall destroy with the brightness of His coming: even Him, whose coming is after the workings of satan with all power and signs and lying wonders, . . ."
> (2 Thessalonians 2: 7-9)

Woe to you, sinners, who are in the midst of the sea and on the land; the reminder against you is evil. Woe to you who acquire gold and silver unjustly and say, "We have become very wealthy, and we have gotten possessions, and we have acquired all that we have wished. And now let us do what we have wished, for silver we have gathered up in our treasuries, and many goods in our houses; and as water they are poured out." You err! For your wealth will not remain, but will quickly ascend from you; for you have acquired everything unjustly, and you will be delivered to a great curse."[5]

"Therefore rejoice, ye heaven, and ye that dwell in them. Woe to the inhabiters of the earth and of the sea! For the devil is come down unto you, having great wrath, because he knoweth that he hath but a short time."

(Revelations 12:12)

The anti-Christ is already on the scene, although he has not yet revealed himself overtly. Almost everyone is paranoid and suspicious of everyone else, even loved ones, all because of these diabolically orchestrated events. **These spiritual vampires have created so much chaos, confusion, despair, and suffering, that most of mankind has been severely distracted from communing with the Father, and seeking His help.**

Mankind is spiraling into an abyss of helplessness, hopelessness and despair; and is so busy attempting to save "things"—houses, cars, jewelry, and provide for their families, that it has been forgotten that God is our source, not man. He created the world and everything in it. He supplies all our needs. Although He knows what we need, we still must ask. God has given us free will and will not interfere or intervene with our choices, without us expressly seeking Him and humbly requesting His help. We need to be asking for gifts of the Spirit, as well as basic earthly needs, not lavish houses, cars, and clothes.

---

[5]   Nickelsburg, George W. E. and Vanderkam, James C., 1 Enoch, (2004) pg. 148

We cannot and must not look to man (the world's hierarchies) to "save" us, their agenda is to utterly destroy us, simply because we are God's, and God loves us! Thus, it is most imperative, in these last days, to put on the full amour of God, as we save souls and build God's army, here on planet earth. God's army is built by providing for basic needs, teaching, preaching, and equipping those who are called. The Holy Spirit informs us of who has been called in preparation for battle.

"Strengthen ye the weak hands and confirm the feeble knees, say to them that are of a fearful heart, be strong, fear not: behold your God will come with vengeance even God with a recompense; He will come and save you."
(Isaiah 35: 3,4)

"And He called unto Him the twelve, and began to send them forth by two and two; and gave them power over unclean spirits."
(Mark 6:7)

"And they overcame him by the Blood of the Lamb, and by the Word of the testimony; and they loved not their lives unto the death."
(Revelations 12:11)

It is very clear that every nation of the world is provoking God to boundless wrath, and continuing in a path of all manner of sin, and outright rebellion, primarily for increased wealth, totalitarian control, and more importantly, to lead God's people into a state of mental turmoil, that we might forget our Father, and our purpose.

The warfare commences in our minds, therefore, keep your mind, and trust, stayed on the Father, Son, and Holy Ghost. Studying the scriptures will reveal how deservedly harsh God dealt with past empires that did not follow his laws and statutes. He will deal with these modern day empires in the same harsh manner. Flagrant sin against the children of God is a reproach and an abomination to God. It is the most rancid stench to His nostrils.

God has given the United States and other industrialized nations the power to obtain wealth and become prosperous. This was done that there might be missionary nations, serving nations less fortunate, and spreading the good news of the Gospel. Those in control of these varying nations have become so greedy, wicked, and selfish, that they don't provide for their own nations, or any other nations. They are behaving as if God in heaven does not exist. Therefore, to them, there is no Supreme Being to be accountable to. When Jesus comes to do battle and judge them, that will be, for them, the future shock! Know that God will not be mocked and will not tolerate such wicked behavior, especially towards His chosen ones, without Divine retribution!

"And He was clothed with a vesture dipped in Blood: and His name is called the Word of God. And the Armies which were in Heaven followed Him upon white horses, clothed in fine linen, white and clean. And out of His mouth goeth a sharp sword, that with it He should smite the nations: And He shall rule them with a rod of iron: and He treadeth the winepress of the fierceness and wrath of Almighty God. And He hath on His vesture and on His thigh a name written, KING OF KINGS, AND LORD OF LORDS."
(Revelations 19: 13-15)

As modern day soldiers, lieutenants, and generals in God's army we must remember that we are in the world, but *not of it*. **This is *not* our home and we must remind ourselves of this fact daily.** We are merely *visitors* awaiting the day and the hour when our Savior, the Redeemer of the World, will come to do battle, free us, and take us home, whether by death or in the twinkling of an eye. Until that time we are commissioned to teach in the four corners of the earth to all who would receive the Good News of the Gospel.

The time is very short, and there is no time to spend an enormous amount of time with one person who is fighting against scripture. Plant the seed, and move on. Come back to water it, to see if it has the potential to produce fruit, if it does not, continue to move on. No point in continuing to water a dead plant! This is a day of warning, not many words! Remind the recipient that is able to receive, about God's forgiveness, God's Word, God's love, and that God supplies all our needs.

When basic human needs are not being met, it is difficult to hear with a spiritual ear. Some can only hear the rumblings of their bellies, or concerned about food and lodging for their children. Satisfy those needs if you are able to, so that the spiritual ear can become opened. In that great day of judgment, may we be blessed to hear, "Well done, thy good and faithful servant".

> "The Christians stood aloof and distinct from the state, as a priestly and Spiritual race, and Christianity seemed able to influence civil life only in that manner which, it must be confessed, is the purest, by practically endeavoring to instill more and more of Holy feeling into the citizens of the state."[6]

How great and marvelous it is to be a soldier in the army of the Lord! Let us not loose sight of the eternal. The things of this earth *shall* pass away. Let our minds, hearts, soul, and spirit stay fixed on Him. It is not the time to be caught up in things, false imaginings, pride, riches, titles, vanity, and lust. Our Father expects us to spread His gospel throughout

---

[6]   Dr. Neader, Agustus, <u>History of the Christian Religion and Church, During the Three First Centuries</u>, translated from the German by H. J. Rose, (1848) pg. 16

the entire world, so that *all* might be saved. This is the Divine assignment for all of us! We must dissolve the "I, me, mine" syndrome. We must be in the role constantly of the good Samaritan, supplying the needs of the people, when we are able to do so, and giving them the Spiritual food—the Word of God, so they, too, are able to grow in Spirit. **They also are the body of Christ, and family.** It is time to be active in the Father's business, and our Christian family's needs in order to build the army. It is time to forsake worldly things and focus on the eternal. We must not keep focused on materials, riches, cars, jewelry, and things we cannot take with us. They are only things, and *will* pass away, and can in no way compare with the heavenly reward the Father has for us, for following His commands and plans. **We must remind ourselves daily that we are only here temporarily, and the events, and the things of this earth are but dust.**

Evil has become a very dominate force in the world, and as a result the world has become a very emotionally cold and desolate place, devoid of natural love and compassion. **This is part of our assignment, to be the light in very dark and cold places, the Light of Christ.**

"But all things that are reproved are made manifest by the Light: for whatsoever doth make manifest is Light. Wherefore He saith, Awake thou that sleepest, and arise from the dead, and Christ shall give thee Light. See then that ye walk circumspectly, not as fools, but as wise, redeeming the time, because the days are evil. Wherefore be ye not unwise, but understanding what the Will of the Lord is. And be not drunk with wine, wherein is excess; but be filled with the Spirit; speaking to yourselves in psalms and hymns and spiritual songs, singing and making melody in you heart to the Lord; giving thanks always for all things unto God and the Father in the Name of our Lord Jesus Christ."

(Ephesians 5:13-20)

It is the best kept secret that mankind has been conditioned and programmed to rely on "the powers that be"—the world's presidents, kings, queens, popes and various other so called political and religious leaders. **The biggest secret is that many of our political and religious leaders are subject to the control of the very evil and powerful, those that are human, as well as those that are evil spirits.** As the elect in the Father's army, we must begin the reconditioning and deprogramming process by teaching and preaching, so that mankind may become fully awake, and aware of the warfare in the spiritual realm. To be forewarned is to be forearmed.

Once it is understood who the enemy really is, and why there is so much wickedness in the world, it can be addressed Spiritually, and affords a level of comfort in knowing that you have the power of God to accomplish this under His instruction. You defeat your enemy by first knowing who he is, and knowing his nature. Then determine what it is he seeks, and to what end. Then contemplate how he will strike out at you, what manner, under what circumstances, and at what time and place.

Study, meditation, and praying in the Spirit will provide these answers. We must pray unceasingly for a move of the Holy Spirit to give us, as well as the new soldiers of the Lord, power! Spiritual ears to hear the word of God and the utterances of the Holy Spirit;

Spiritual minds to comprehend, Spiritual eyes to see and recognize the "illuminated" evil, anti-Christ, and anything not of God; Spiritual limbs to move to do the work of the Father; and Spiritual mouths to speak Gospel Truth to all who will listen. Thank you Holy Ghost for guidance, comfort, and gifts and fruits of the Spirit.

"Thou hast also given me the necks of mine enemies, that I might destroy them that hate me."
(2 Samuel 22: 41)

THE SPIRITUAL ANOINTING OF GOD

"That which is born of the Spirit is spirit."
(John 3:6)

"The Lord tested them much, and their spirits were found true, so that they might bless His name."
(1 Enoch 108:9)[7]

"While Peter yet spake these words, the Holy Ghost fell on all them which heard the Word. And they of the circumcision which believed were astonished, as many as came with Peter, because that on the Gentiles also was poured out the Gift of the Holy Ghost. For they heard them speak with tongues, and magnify God"
(Acts 10:44-46)

"But the anointing which ye have received of Him abideth in you, and ye need not that any man should teach you: but as the

---

[7]   Nickelsburg George W. E. and VanderKam, James C. 1 Enoch, (2004), pg. 169

same Anointing teacheth you of all things, and is truth, and no
lie, and even as It hath taught you, ye shall abide in Him."
(1 John 2:27)

The Spiritual Anointing of God is the ultimate Spiritual gift of the Holy
Spirit. These gifts manifest as the Holy Spirit grants them, for whatever
spiritual necessity that arises. Some are gifted to be preachers, teachers,
apostles, evangelists, prophets, tongues, discerning of tongues, prophecy,
wisdom, miracles, and healings. The gifts of the Holy Spirit are freely
given, yet must be earned by living according to God's expectations, and
with obedience, prayer and fasting. Some teach that you are only able to
receive one or two gifts. This is not true. The Spirit gives the gifts that
are needed for any circumstance and at any time. Don't put limits on the
Holy Spirit, or place Him in a box. The Holy Spirit is limitless! As we
begin to increasingly grow in the Spirit, and be used for His purpose, this
truth will manifest.

"But the manifestation of the Spirit is given to every man to
profit withal. For one is given by the Spirit the word of wisdom;
to another the word of knowledge by the same Spirit; to another
faith by the same Spirit; to another the gifts of healing by the
same Spirit; to another the working of miracles; to another
prophecy; to another discerning of spirits; to another of divers
kinds of tongues; to another the interpretation of tongues: But
all these worketh that One and the Selfsame Spirit, dividing to
every man severally as He wills."
(1 Corinthians 12: 7-11)

In our stages of spiritual growth we should become more conscious of our
righteousness in Jesus, as opposed to our sin as mere man. Practicing a
consciousness of righteousness is a journey in becoming spiritually mature.
The growth process of maturity in the Spirit does not have to be tedious

or painful, but it has to be sought reverently, consistently, and humbly with obedience, and prayer.

Under the law, man was conscious of his sin continually; but under the New Covenant God desires for us to focus more on who we are, and what we have in Christ Jesus. Our own righteousness is filthy in His sight. As we grow to please Him, we become more aware of our new creation realities. These realities are more powerful than the bonds of sin, because sin is no longer our master. We are not under the law, but under grace.[8]

> "For sin shall not have dominion over you, for you are not under the law but under grace."
> (Romans 6:14)

> "I write to you, little children, because your sins are forgiven you for His name's sake. I write to you, fathers, because you have known Him Who is from the beginning. I write to you young men, because you have overcome the wicked one. I write to you little children, because you have known the Father. I have written to you, fathers, because you have known Him Who is from the beginning. I have written to you, young men, because you are strong, and the Word of God abides in you, and you have overcome the wicked one."
> (1 John 2: 12-14)

God is a Spirit, and gives the Fruit of the Spirit and the Gifts of the Spirit. Therefore, we must, understand the Nature of God as the Holy Spirit reveals it to us. We must be an open vessel, extending an invitation for the Holy Spirit to enter and guide our lives and our ministries. **We must surrender *all*, and *completely* to *His Will* and *His Way*. Most importantly, all that is done must be done *for the Glory of God.*** It is very tempting and easy to boast, "I healed . . . ., or I imparted . . . ., or

---

8   Dr. Bailey, Patricia, <u>Step into Divine Destiny</u>, (2003), pgs. 49-53

I preached so well." Don't ever be guilty of competing with God for His glory, because without Him we can do nothing well or in righteousness. Our prayer should be "Father *use me* for Your Glory, I don't want or need Your glory, I just want and need Your love, and to be pleasing in Your sight, a sweet fragrance to Your nostrils, a delight to Your heart." Let us continue to grow in the knowledge of God and His plan for our lives in the midst of this spiritual battle. When we have become aware of our assignment, then is the time to implement *everything* Father God has commissioned us to do.

> "The oath which He sware to our father Abraham, that He would grant unto us, that we being delivered out of the hand of our enemies might serve Him without fear, in Holiness and righteousness before Him, all the days of our life.
> (Luke 1: 73-75)

Many of us have experienced growth pains during our journey to spiritual evolvement. This is not by chance; our lives are driven by purpose. Even in the darkest clouds there are silver linings. That silver lining is the spiritual lesson learned from each event. Each life experience, the good, the bad, and the ugly, is necessary to bring us to the place where we are appreciative and are worthy to be a recipient of the Holy Spirit, and to be able to teach with a testimony.

Many of us need a testimony in order to demonstrate the Greatness and Mercy of God while teaching others. We share these life experiences to show God's forgiveness, grace, mercy and unconditional love; as well as the move of the Holy Spirit in getting us back on a righteous path. We remind our people that if He has done it for me, He will also do it for you, because He is no respecter of persons.

Many people are so self condemned that they see themselves as extremely unworthy of God's love, protection, mercy, and forgiveness, or unworthy to be a recipient of the gifts and fruits of the Holy Spirit, and unworthy to become a part of God's family. If we once lived in a manner that resembles their present existence, we need to let them know this. The recipients of the teaching often need a testimony in order to realize that we have shared experiences with some of the same trials of life, and we also, once fell short of the Glory of God. Most important, this makes it known that our Father is a God of extreme love, mercy and forgiveness.

"When He shall come to be glorified in His saints, and to be admired in all them that believe (because our testimony among you was believed) in that day. Wherefore also we pray always for you, that our God would count you worthy of this calling, and fulfill all the good pleasure of His goodness, and the work of faith with power. That the name of our Lord Jesus Christ may be glorified in you, and ye in Him, according to the Grace of our God and the Lord Jesus Christ.

(2 Thessalonians 1: 10-12)

Living, breathing testimony demonstrates the Greatness and Mercy of God. He loves all of us unconditionally, and even when we're in a sin state. Each negative event in a person's life is not of God, and are instruments of evil to keep the people wallowing in a mire of self condemnation. With this state of mind, a person cannot even talk to God, they feel too ashamed and unworthy. We must lift them up, remind them of the Atonement of Jesus, God's love, mercy, and forgiveness, and teach them the good fight, spiritual warfare!

"Behold, I give unto you power to tread on serpents and scorpions, and over all the power of the enemy: and nothing shall by any means hurt you."

(Luke 10:19)

God would not give us power to tread on the devil and his minions, and then permit them to overtake us. With this power we must make changes in the world, and in the lives of those we encounter, as we pass through this existence. We have been provided with all the equipment necessary to accomplish this under the guidance of the Holy Spirit. We have been given power over and above any demon. The sacrifice of Jesus has made this a reality. (The atonement is real!!!) Jesus has *already* defeated satan by His Work on the Cross! It is fruitless, to *have* the power, yet not make use of it. No doubt the devil delights in this, and scourges the situation all the more.

We cannot afford to play around with our problems or the problems of others, wasting time, and missing the Holy Spirits timing for solving them. The Holy Spirit convicts the world of righteousness, (sin), and judgment. "And when He is come, He will reprove the world of righteousness, (sin), and of judgment . . ." (Jn 16: 8). The word "reprove" is variously translated in different versions as: convince, convict, expose, and rebuke. Someone has stated: "These three things are the most difficult to impress on any man, for he can always attempt to justify himself by asserting an excusable motive for evil actions, or by pleading a relative scale of ethical standards in the place of absolute righteousness, or by assuming that judgment is indefinitely deferred so that it is no real threat." (The authors are indebted to the unknown source of this quote.) Only the Holy Spirit can overcome the blindness and deceitfulness of the sinful, human heart and make a man realize the greatness of his own iniquity. Notice the particular sin of which the Holy Spirit will convict. It is not the sin of stealing, drunkenness or adultery. Conscience will convict a man that such things are wrong, but the Holy Spirit convicts of a sin of which conscience would never convict him—the sin of unbelief. Unbelief of Jesus Christ is the greatest of all sins, for it causes the rejection of God's only means of forgiveness, and thus brings all the condemnation of one's every sin upon the one who fails to appropriate Christ's salvation through faith.[9] The only greater and *unforgiveable* sin is grieving the Holy Spirit.

---

[9]   Duffield, Guy P. and Van Cleave, Nathaniel M., <u>Foundations of Pentecostal Theology</u>, (1987), pg. 26

God has given us free will, to believe, or not to believe; free will to seek the Holy Spirit, or not to. However, if we desire the Holy Spirit's power, we must get out of God's way, and allow the Spirit to move in any situation as He sees fit. The Holy Spirit can and will resolve any situation so much more than we could ever contemplate or dream of. While we're trying to figure it out, God has already worked it out in the midnight hour. If God's dunamis power has been quenched because of our life choices, it is now time to make changes that give Him free reign within us. Are you hindering or enabling God to do want He wants to do through you? Only we can disable the power of God in our lives, based on our unsavory life choices. Ungodly behavior will disable the power of God in our lives. Ungodly lifestyles render the Holy Spirit powerless to move in our lives and in our circumstances. He will not dwell in an unclean temple, participate in unclean acts, nor accompany us to unclean places.

God has allowed us to decide the type of lifestyle we desire. He will not intervene in our choices because He has given us agency, or free will. Whatever is sown will be reaped. The good, bad, and ugly will produce fruit of its own kind in your life. The negative you put out will return to you, and so will the good. So do make choices that are right, just, true, and give glory to God. We don't have to live a lifestyle of mediocrity, stagnation, and defeat. We don't have to be ruled by negative circumstances, and we don't have to feel powerless in the face of increasing evil, governmental inadequacies and corruption, conspiracy theories, oil spills, the rumblings of the earth, and seemingly never ending despair. We must stir up the gifts of the Spirit. God has a system in place that permits us to build ourselves up. That system is praying in the Holy Spirit daily, so the Spirit of God will dominate our lives. The fears, emotions, and fleshly erroneous reasoning's *will* dissipate.

". . . stir up the gift of God, which is in thee . . ."
(2 Timothy 1:6)

Fear is an acronym (false evidence appearing real). In other words, a lie straight from the pit of hell. Negative emotions can be painful or numbing, and human reasoning's can lead us to paths, leading to destruction. With the gifts of the Spirit, we can see the enemy through God's eyes, and can look him square in the eye without fear or intimidation. We will then recognize that he is but an annoying fly. **With the power of the Holy Ghost and by the Blood of Jesus, when we tell him to go, *he must go*; and add, with the Authority of the Holy Spirit, that he is to go to outer darkness, *never* to return, or be reassigned again!!!** Yes!! When we have the Holy Ghost, we have that kind of power!!! It is more than empowering to have the Power of the Holy Ghost, but we must be able to use that power without fear, intimidation, or any of our human reasoning's. After all, it is the Holy Ghost's Power, not ours; so what is there to fear!?

"Therefore, brethren, we comforted over you in all our affliction and distress by your faith: For now we live, if ye stand fast in the Lord. For what thanks can we render to God again for you, for all the joy wherewith we joy for your sakes before our God; Night and day praying exceedingly that we might see your face and might perfect that which is lacking in your faith? Now God Himself and our Father, and our Lord Jesus Christ, direct our way unto you."

(1 Thessalonians 3: 7-11)

The Holy Spirit is a person. He does see you, hear you, and talk to you. He will meet you right where you are, if you seek Him. He will convict you when you sin, and He will purify you, and anoint you, but only if you desire it. Without the Holy Spirit, one is open to, and vulnerable to *any* and *all* demonic activity. This, of course, will throw a person into rebellion, debauchery, and every manner of sin; and further and further away from the Spirit of God, and often without knowing *how* they got there! You have authority through the power of God in you, to overcome the works of the devil, his kingdom of darkness and despair, and all of his demonic authority. However, you must use Holy Ghost authority or you, and world around you will never change, and can become a vessel for all manner of evil. When you are in tuned with the Holy Spirit, through His power you can change situations and circumstances despite the wiles of the enemy. It is a part of the battle strategy of our Father.

"Finally, my brethren, be strong in the Lord, and in the power of his might. Put On the whole armor of God, that ye may be able to stand against the wiles of the devil. For we wrestle not against flesh and blood, but against principalities, against powers, against the rulers of the darkness of this world, against spiritual wickedness in high places. Wherefore take unto you the whole amour of God, that ye may be able to withstand in the evil day, and having done all, to stand.

(Ephesians 6: 1-14)

What can be said about the Almighty Father? There are no earthly words to describe His goodness, mercy, grace, and unconditional love. These are only a very few attributes of our Father, but unconditional love is one of the most important. God loves us, and He loves us unconditionally. He even loves us when we're in a state of sin. He's not happy about it, disappointed, and sometimes angry, but He still loves us nonetheless; and has great expectation that we will return to His love. This is unconditional love.

"Return to Me," declares the Lord Almighty, "and I will return to you."

(Zechariah 1:3) (NIV)

"Because he hath set his love upon Me, therefore will I deliver him: I will set him on high, because he hath known My Name. He shall call upon Me, and I will answer him: I will be with him in trouble; I will deliver him, and honor him. With long life will I satisfy him, and shew him My salvation."

(Psalm 91: 16)

Our Father knows our nature, He created us. He knows we will sin, but it is His desire for us to strive to be more like Jesus. That is why He sent Him, as the Perfect Example. The more we strive to be like Jesus, the more sin becomes alienated from us, and we become closer to our Father, and receive more of the gifting of the Holy Spirit. It is then that He will impart His anointing, and the Holy Ghost will dwell within us. How comforting and reassuring it is to know that the Holy Ghost lives in us, and is with us always, when we're obedient. **With true Holy Ghost power, no demon in all of hell can harm us. No demon in all of hell dares to even *look* in our direction.** When we become generals, lieutenants, and soldiers in God's army, we are armed and prepared for battle. We go out two by two, to bring in the lost, forgotten, hopeless and the spiritually bankrupt. We share the knowledge of God's grace, mercy, forgiveness, and unconditional love. **We assist the lost in returning to the Father with prayers of repentance, communing with those who strive to be like Jesus, and unshakable faith in God's ability to change us.** We share the knowledge of Holy Ghost power and what the full amour of God is. The Holy Spirit convicts us, purifies us, protects us, anoints us, and strengthen us to do battle against the wicked. He is faithful to those who know Him, love Him, and seek Him unceasingly.

"Beloved, now are we the sons of God, and it doth not yet appear what we shall be: but we know that, when He shall appear, we shall be like Him; for we shall see Him as He is. And every man that hath this hope in Him purifieth himself, even as He is pure."

(1 John 3: 2,3)

"Each one should use whatever gift he has received to serve others, faithfully administering God's Grace in its various forms."

(1 Peter 4:10) (NIV)

Commune with the Father all the day long, with minute prayers of love, thanksgiving, and praise. Make Him a part of your every day walk. Share with Him your thoughts, feelings, and concerns, and seek His advisement throughout the day. In the evening, pray continuously with a contrite heart, and revel in His peace, joy, and love. Surely this will keep you on the straight and narrow path that leads to righteousness and exceeding joy, despite all the worlds difficulties around you. **There is peace when in communion with God, peace of mind, peace of heart, and peace of spirit. There is also unspeakable joy that surpasses all understanding.**

When mankind is stressing, living in despair, and totally hopeless, tell them no matter what the circumstance is, **God is *STILL* in control, and able to create miracles in our lives!** His abilities to move in our situations are limitless, to those who know and love Him, follow His statutes, commune with Him, and believe and trust that He is all knowing and all powerful!

"I have been young, and now am old; yet have I not seen the righteous forsaken nor his seed begging bread."
(Psalm 37: 25)

"The righteous eateth to the satisfying of his soul: but the belly of the wicked shall want."
(Proverbs 13: 25)

"So when they had dined, Jesus saith to Simon Peter, Simon, son of Jonas, lovest thou me more than these? He saith unto Him, yea, Lord; thou knowest that I love Thee. He saith unto him, feed My lambs. He saith to him again the second time, Simon, son of Jonas, love thou Me? He saith unto Him, yea, Lord; thou knowest that I love Thee. He saith unto him, feed My sheep."
(John 21: 15, 16)

There it is. These, and several other scriptures let us know that our Father supplies all of our needs, and expects us to supply the needs of others when we can. He feeds the birds of the air; how much more you? When we follow His statutes and commands, He is faithful to provide all that we need, and some! How wonderful it is to know that we have a Heavenly Father Who is always there for us in any and every circumstance. All we need do is call His Name reverently and lovingly. He will answer, and satisfy us with desires of our hearts, that are in keeping with His Will.

> "Every good gift and every perfect gift is from above, and cometh down from the Father of Lights, with Whom is no variableness, neither shadow of turning."
> (James 1:17)

Discernment is defined as keenly selective judgment; not in the sense of judging a person or thing, but in determining the nature of a person or thing. In the natural, it is what we call the sixth sense, or intuition. We use this sixth sense for example, to determine if a job is right for us, or if a particular person is worthy to be called friend, or if it's going to rain according to our "intuitive" aches and pains. It is something we use in our every day walk in life, and it may prove to be true, or not. It is not always reliable. It is most often unreliable because it is something that is practiced in the flesh. As imperfect fleshly beings, anything we produce in the flesh is also imperfect; and it is imperative that we learn to rely on the gift of Spiritual discernment from the Holy Spirit in all of His perfection.

> "And my speech and my preaching was not with enticing words of man's wisdom, but in demonstration of the Spirit of Power: that your faith should not stand in the wisdom of men, but in the Power of God. Howbeit we speak wisdom among them that are perfect: yet not the wisdom of this world, nor of the princes of this world, that come to naught: but we speak the Wisdom of God in a mystery, even the hidden Wisdom,

which God ordained before the world unto our glory: which none of the princes of this world knew: For had they known it, they would not have crucified the Lord of Glory. But as it is written, eye hath not seen, nor ear heard, neither have it entered into the heart of man, the things which God hath prepared for them that love Him. But God hath revealed them unto us by His Spirit: for the Spirit searcheth all things, yea, the Deep Things of God."

(1 Corinthians 2: 4)

We must continuously make a conscious effort to follow the commands of the Lord and refrain from sin, so that we may prove worthy to receive the gifts of the Holy Spirit. This includes repenting of all our sins, past, present, and future, abstaining from sin, and anything, any place, and any person associated with it. With the gift of the Spirit comes all the gifts and fruits associated with Him, even the gift of Spiritual discernment.

This is Spiritual wisdom.

"Now we have received, not the spirit of the world, but the Spirit which is of God; that we might know the things that are freely given to us of God. Which things also we speak, not in the words which man's wisdom teacheth, but which the Holy Ghost teacheth; comparing Spiritual things with Spiritual: But the natural man receiveth not the things of the Spirit of God: for they are foolishness unto him: neither can he know them, because they are Spiritually discerned."

(1Corinthians 2: 12-14)

Wisdom that is birthed from self serving interests, is diabolical in contrast to Spiritual wisdom from above. Godly wisdom exemplifies the fruit of the Spirit. God is so wise in His dealings with men, that He gave us *Spiritual intuition* to decipher between Heavenly and earthly wisdom. We can test this wisdom by asking ourselves the following questions: Is this wisdom peaceable and loveable, or does it leave us with contentions and hatreds: Is this wisdom pure or full of hypocrisy, partiality, and self serving in nature? Is this wisdom willing to share, and is it full of mercy.

THE GIFT
OF SPIRITUAL DISCERNMENT

"Make sure of all things; hold fast to what is fine."
(1 Thessalonians 5:21)

When we are learning to be led by the Wisdom of the Holy Spirit, we must never overlook our God-given indicators. We sometimes compromise these indicators in our life with excuses and justifications. We should separate our emotions from the indicators of God because He will not lead us by using our emotions. The number one way of frustrating our human spirit, and making circumstances far worse, is involving and depending upon our emotions in deciding the actions we should take. Emotions are always temporary, fickle, and subject to change. Let's think of our emotions as whipped cream. When we begin to judge spiritual matters with our whipped cream-like emotions, temporary and changeable whipped cream will not be able to hold up against heat, wind, and pressure. It is only a surface topping to give an attractive appearance.[10] And so it is with our battle with the enemy! It is not the time to be ill prepared, revved up on worldly events, hoping to acquire the "things" of the world, immersed in our personal circumstances, and especially not losing sight of our anointing and the battle plan!

---

[10] Dr. Bailey, Patricia, <u>Step into Divine Destiny</u>, (2003), pg. 212

We must not rely on human imaginings, teachings, and emotions. **Remember we are imperfect fleshly beings. We must always rely on the unction, utterances, and groanings of the Holy Spirit, Who is perfect in all His Ways.**

"Likewise the Spirit also helpeth our infirmities: for we know not what we should pray for as we ought: But the Spirit itself maketh intercession for us with groanings which cannot be uttered. And He that searcheth the hearts knoweth what is the mind of the Spirit, because He maketh intercession for the saints according to the Will of God. And we know that all things work together for good to them that love God, to them who are called according to His purpose. For whom He did foreknow, He also did predestinate to be conformed to the Image of His Son, that He might be the Firstborn among many brethren. Moreover whom He did predestinate, them He also called: and whom He called, them He also justified: and whom He justified, them He also glorified.

(Romans 8: 26-30)

We need Holy Ghost power because it is without a doubt that satan, son of perdition, is the prince of this world. The increase in wars, violence, political and social unrest, unnecessary death, rape, torture, and murder, ecological upheavals and destruction, and economic collapse are prevalent in the world today—and escalating with an uncanny frequency. The frequency with which earthquakes, tsunamis, and economic collapse around the world is occurring is a grave indication that time is tight and satan is running scared because he knows his time is very short. Mankind has lost faith in it's governing earthly hierarchies, but continues to look to them, nonetheless, for hope for a better tomorrow, while being shackled by the trappings of this world. It is inconceivable to most, that these governing bodies could fail, and let the planet spiral out of control. Whatever could be the matter?

All of the worlds top governing officials belong to secret societies, who have covert agendas, and themselves are governed by an elitist few who constantly play chess with the lives of the "little people" for incessantly and insanely increasing wealth, power, and world domination. These, in turn, are under the power of the son of perdition. The steel companies, oil companies, all of big business corporations, and makers of weapons of war, exceed abundantly in finances, in the midst of war. There is no wonder that there are always wars, and rumors of war. The hospitals, pharmaceutical companies, medical equipment companies, insurance companies, and health care officials are all in bed together, prescribing unnecessary medications and treatments for monetary gain, not treating those who are indigent, and providing substandard care, for those who do have insurance, especially medicare. This wicked idolatry—the love of money, at the suffering of the masses, has become their god, and they do not know God Almighty.

> "For all that is in the world, the lust of the flesh, and the lust of the eyes, and the pride of life, is not of the Father, but is of the world."
>
> 1 John 2:16)

(These are multi-billionaires, and a few trillionaires, yet the desire for more wealth is like an empty void that can never be filled.) The world's billionaires have gained 1.2 trillion in collective net worth since 2009, and now 56 countries have at least one billionaire among their citizens.[11] Take note that this is in addition to the billions they already had. Interestingly enough, this increase in wealth occurred somewhere around all the world's financial crises, subprime loans, failing housing market, failing economy, out sourcing of jobs, increased unemployment, lack of health insurance, and inadequate health care, just to name a few. Simply stated, the world's financial crises, was a prelude to their increase in wealth. The rich, stealing from the poor, perhaps!? **Obviously the very wealthy have become**

---

[11]   www.askville.amgon.om/billionaires-world/AnswerView

wealthier, while the working class is closer to acquiring third world status.

> "For in one hour so great riches is come to nought. And every shipmaster, and all the company in ships, and sailors, and as many as trade by sea, stood afar off, and cried when they saw the smoke of her burning, saying, what city is like unto this great city! And they cast dust on their heads, and cried, weeping and wailing, saying, alas, alas, that great city, wherein were made rich all that had ships in the sea by reason of her costliness! For in one hour is she made desolate. Rejoice over her, thou heaven, and ye Holy apostles and prophets; for God hath avenged you on her.
> (Revelations 18: 17-20)

One must wonder, with so much wealth in the world, why are there so many problems compounding and compounding—famine, unnecessary deaths for need of treatment and medication, abject poverty, populated barren lands, homelessness, wars . . . . and the list goes on. It is because of the self serving greediness, stinginess, and wickedness of a very few at the very top. It is the "little people," the middle class, and lower class, who are suffering, and require ministry the most. The rich, no doubt, probably feel they definitely don't need it (although they do) and probably definitely don't desire it. Money and material riches, a type of idolatry, is their god. In fact, their very souls are in slavery to it, to the detriment of their own salvation. They cannot see beyond the riches, and care not who suffers in order that they may have more, and more. They have been deceived by the evil one to believe that this life is all there is. Therefore, for them, there can be no devil, no hell, no eternal punishment.

> "And I saw an angel come down from heaven, having the key of the bottomless pit and a great chain in his hand. And he laid hold on the dragon, that old serpent, which is the devil, and

satan, and bound him a thousand years, and cast him into the bottomless pit, and shut him up, and set a seal upon him, that he should deceive the nations no more, till the thousand years should be fulfilled: and after that he must be loosed a little season.

(Revelations 20: 1-3)

It is rather sad, when you think about it, that these people believe that what you have, defines who you are. This, of course, is satanic thinking. And they think the more you have, the greater and more powerful you are. However the draw back is that they are devoid of Spirit. They have no concept of human kindness, compassion, family, community, and a loving Father, Creator of all. It obviously is not in their DNA, nor are they part of God's family! Their existence is based only on this earth plane, and for them, there is nothing beyond it.

"Every one that is proud in heart is an abomination to the Lord: though hand in hand, he shall not be unpunished."
(Proverbs 16:5)

Biblical text states that, it is easier for a camel to pass through the eye of a needle, than for a rich man to enter into the Kingdom of Heaven. Why? There must be some continuous wickedness involved with acquiring, maintaining, and continually progressing in wealth, while so many others are in abject poverty, and suffering as a result. Very few of the rich have the mindset or heart, to help others who are less fortunate, in poverty and squalor, and endure immense suffering on a daily basis. The Robin Hood concept is no longer in operation. It is just the opposite—the rich *taking, and taking* from the poor, and quickly dwindling the middle class into unwarranted poverty, with tent cities stretching across the nation, and famine, sickness, and death following closely behind!

.

"Hearken, my beloved brethren, hath not God chosen the poor
of this world rich in faith, and heirs of the Kingdom which He
hath promised to them that love Him? But ye have despised the
poor. Do not rich men oppress you, and draw you before the
judgment seats? Do not they blaspheme that Worthy Name by
the which ye are called?"

(James 2: 5-7)

(While our nation's attention is drawn to scandals in Washington, and
scandals of Hollywood, the whole world around us is falling deeper and
deeper into financial ruin.) Russian is starving. Asia is lost in a dark hole
of despair. South Korea is on the brink of chaos. China faces financial
ruin, with millions of people already unemployed, hungry, and homeless.
Now South America is beginning to disintegrate. And as the nations begin
falling like dominoes, the international monetary fund quakes with fear,
because its resources are nearly gone. I tell you, what is happening cannot
be fixed. There is no magic bullet to save us. God is about to chasten the
nations of the world through an economic holocaust—and His sword is
already unsheathed![12]

"And after these things I saw another angel come down from
heaven, having great power; and the earth was lightened with
his glory. And he cried mightily with a strong voice, saying,
Babylon the great is fallen, is fallen, and is become the habitation
of devils, and the hold of every foul spirit, and a cage of every
unclean and hateful bird. For all nations have drunk of the
wine of the wrath of her fornication, and the kings of the earth
have committed fornication with her, and the merchants of the
earth are waxed rich through the abundance of her delicacies.
And I heard another voice from heaven, saying, come out of
her, my people, that ye be not partakers of her sins, and that

[12]   Wilkerson, David, God's Plan to Protect His People in the Coming
Depression, (1998), pg. 2

ye receive not of her plagues. For her sins have reached unto
heaven, and God hath remembered her iniquities.

(Revelation 18: 1-5)

So, why do so many pastors continue to promote prosperity teachings!?
Some teach in their own "wisdom", and for others, it has to do with
numbers in the congregation and keeping the "tithes" ("their" money)
elevated regardless of the truth. Sadly, many ministers are unaware of the
direct correlation of a world in crisis, (how and why it got there, God's plan
concerning it,) and the steadily increasing wealth of the very wicked few
at the very top. These ministers and preachers foolishly go about teaching
"prosperity" doctrines (their prosperity, quiet as it is kept) and tickle your
ear sermons. This is priest craft (witchcraft in the church). Know that this
is an abomination before our Father, and the payment for such a crime
against God's people—and God, is just unfathomable. It is now the time
to preach the truth of what God has said about these times—the fate of
the wicked, and the fate of the faithful, and to keep our eyes on Him,
despite the events happening all around us. It is now the time to know our
Father's voice, and another we shall never follow. Forget about having the
(earthly) mansion, the jewels, the lamborghini, the furs, and the designer
clothes. This is all vanity and will come to dust!

"An high look, and a proud heart, and the plowing of the
wicked, is sin."

(Proverbs 21:4)

"For they loved the praise of men more than the praise of
God."

(John 12:43)

"Thou saidist, I shall be a lady for ever: so that thou didst
not lay these things to thy heart, neither didst remember the
latter end of it. Therefore hear now this, thou that are given to
pleasures that dwellest carelessly, that sayest in thine heart, I

am, and none else beside me; I shall not sit as a widow, neither shall know the loss of children: "But these two things shall come to thee in a moment in one day, the loss of children; and widowhood: they shall come upon thee in their perfection for the multitude of thy sorceries, and for the great abundance of thine enchantments.

(Isaiah 47: 7-9)

(Our country and the world is in the greatest depression of our times, although the powers that be, refuse to say the "D" word). What was it, exactly, that shook America and the world (during the time of the Great Depression of 1929), turning prosperity to poverty overnight? What brought on that world wide depression? Simply put, it was the LORD. It was the same God who destroyed Sodom and Gomorrah for their sins . . . the same God Who judged Israel for its idolatry, bringing Titus' army down on Jerusalem to destroy it. The same God Who promises in Revelations to wipe out the prosperity of Babylon in a single hour . . . the same God Who has been warning America about its sin for years, through the voices of prophets who cry out with grieving, broken hearts.[13] Yes, America *is* modern day Babylon.

". . . And I saw a woman sit upon a scarlet colored beast, full of names of blasphemy, having seven heads and ten horns. And the woman was arrayed in purple and scarlet colour, and decked with gold and precious stones and pearls, having a golden cup in her hand full of abominations and filthiness of her fornication: and upon her forehead was a name written, MYSTERY BABYLON THE GREAT, THE MOTHER OF HARLOTS AND ABOMINATIONS OF THE EARTH. And I saw the woman drunken with the blood of the saints, and with the blood of the martyrs of Jesus: . . . ."

(Revelation 17: 3-6)

---

[13] www.religiononline.org

"And the woman which thou sawest is that great city, which reigneth over the kings of the earth."
(Revelation 17: 18)

"For thou has trusted in thy wickedness; thou hast said, none seeth me. Thy wisdom and thy knowledge, it hath perverted thee: and thou has said in thine heart, I am, and none else beside me. Therefore evil shall come upon thee; thou shalt not know from whence it riseth; and mischief shall fall upon thee; thou shalt not be able to put if off; and desolation shall come upon thee suddenly, which thou shalt not know."
(Isaiah 47: 10-11)

"Humble yourselves therefore under the Mighty Hand of God, that He may exalt you in due time: Casting all your care upon Him; for He careth for you. Be sober, be vigilant; because your adversary the devil, a roaring lion, walketh about seeking whom he may devour: Whom resist steadfast in the faith, knowing that the same afflictions are accomplished in your brethren that are in the world. But the God of all Grace, Who hath called us unto His Eternal Glory by Christ Jesus, after that ye have suffered a while, make you perfect, stablish, strengthen, settle you.
(1Peter 5: 6-10)

With all the wickedness around us in the world today, one may wonder how wickedness entered the world in the first place. We know Adam and Eve were made in God's image and according to His likeness, therefore, there could be no wickedness within them, they were simply misguided by the serpent. The Book of Enoch, which was conveniently abolished by the early church "fathers," sheds light on the corruption of corporeal angels, their deeds, their fall, and as a result, how wickedness entered the world.

In the guise and garb of Christian and Jew, "they"—the fallen angels and those who they influenced—denounced and suppressed the Book of

Enoch's record of the fall of angels through the lusts of the flesh. Their verdicts of heresy and blasphemy rested against Enoch for over fifteen hundred years.[14]

The materiality of angels seems to have been an age-old belief. There was the angel with whom Jacob wrestled—physical enough to cripple him at least temporarily, if not for life. So tangible was this angel that the author of the Book of Genesis calls him a man, although elsewhere Scripture reveals that he was an angel. The 'angel' said to Jacob, "Let me go, for the day breaketh." How could Jacob have had hold upon an incorporeal angel? The angels who came to visit Sodom had to be bolted indoors in Lot's house in order to protect them from an intended sexual assault by local townspeople—sodomites who wanted to get to "know" the angels. And Manoah offered to cook dinner for his guest—presumed to be an ordinary man until he ascended to heaven in the fire Manoah had. Only then did Manoah know that the "man of God" was an angel of the Lord.[15]

The angels or "watchers" themselves, mingled with the daughters of men, and used the Great Knowledge entrusted to them to establish an order of things on earth in direct contradiction to what was intended by God . . . God is angry in their attempts to surpass His power . . . They came together and created the antimimon pneuma, a clever imitation of the true order of things, "and they brought gold and silver, and metals, copper, and iron, and all the treasures of the earth, so they married the women and begat the children of darkness; their hearts were closed up, and they became hard by this imitation false spirit." **It was the deliberate exploitation of the heavenly order as a franchise for sordid earthly ambitions . . . This vicious order was riveted down by solemn oaths and covenants . . . When the Sons of Heaven marry the daughters of the sons of men, (with) their leader semiazus . . .** [16]

---

[14]   Prophet, Elizabeth Clare, <u>Fallen Angels and Origins of Evil</u>, (2000), pg. 68

[15]   Prophet, Elizabeth Clare, <u>Fallen Angels and Origins of Evil</u>, (2000), pgs. 7, 8

[16]   Nibley, Hugh, <u>Enoch The Prophet</u>, (1986), pgs. 8-10

The wickedness of Enoch's day had a special stamp and flavor; only the most determined and entrenched depravity merited the extermination of the race. In apocryphal Enoch stories we are told how humanity was let to the extremes of misconduct under the tutelage of uniquely competent masters. According to these traditions, these were none other than special heavenly messengers who were sent down to earth to restore respect for the name of God among the degenerate human race but instead yielded to temptation, misbehaved with the daughters of men, and ended up instructing and abetting their human charges in all manner of iniquity. They are variously designated as the watchers, fallen angels, sons of God, nephilim, or rephaim, and are sometimes confused with their offspring, the giants . . . **"Why have you left heaven [and] the Exalted One," says Enoch in a Gizeh fragment, "and . . . with the daughters of men defiled yourselves? . . . Ye have behaved as sons of Earth and begotten to yourselves giant sons. And you were once holy, spiritual, eternal beings . . . and have lusted after the flesh . . . as do mortal and perishable creatures." What made the world of Enoch so singularly depraved, as to invite total obliteration, was the deliberate and systematic perversion of heavenly things to justify wickedness.**[17]

So, you see *why* it is so important to stay aware of what's going on around you in the flesh and in the spirit, decipher the motives of all people (are they God's children?) especially clergy (your soul salvation is at stake!), and especially government leaders (who care nothing about you!), and themselves are puppets, receiving orders from *wickedness in high places*!

If we acknowledge that, in fact, there does exist a power far greater than the elected office of the president, a "moral" authority far more powerful than the Christian pope, an invisible power that controls the world's military apparatus and intelligence systems, controls the international banking system, controls the most effective propaganda system in history, we might be then forced to conclude that democracy (and freedom) is, at best, an illusion, and at worst, a prelude to a dictatorship (controlled and manipulated by secret societies that will usher in the New World Order).[18]

---

[17]   Nibley, Hugh, <u>Enoch The Prophet</u>, (1986), pgs. 178-180

[18]   Estulin, Daniel, <u>The True Story of the Bilderberg Group</u>, (2007), pg. 63

These evil ones include, but are not limited to, the illuminati, the council on foreign relation, the trilateral commission, the federal reserve, skull and bones, the bilderberg group, and the freemasons, to name only a very few. **One should surmise that they are of the "satanic bloodline."** Let that marinate for a moment.

"Some nations place the sovereignty of their land in the hands of a single ruler

(monarchy), some in the hands of a small number of rulers (oligarchy), and some in the hands of the people (democracy). Moses our teacher taught us to place our faith in none of these forms of government. He taught us to obey the rule of God, for to God alone did he accord kingship and power. He commanded the people always to raise their eyes to God, for He is the source of all good for mankind in general and for each person in particular and in Him will people find help when they pray to Him in their time of suffering, for no act is hidden from His understanding and no hidden thought of man's heart is hidden from Him"

Josephus Flavius, Contra Apion, Volume One[19]

As soldiers in God's army we must stand firm and resolute in honoring our God with obedience to His Divine plan for the salvation of all. Work your assignment to the glory of God. Listen for the small still voice of the Holy Spirit to guide and direct us through these very dark days of hidden agendas, and plans of destruction for the children of the Lord. **Always remember God** *is still in control!!!* Remember and perform your assignment in the Army of Jesus, Majestic Conquering Lion of Judah! Give praise, honor, and glory to our heavenly Father always. **Pray always in the Spirit with a pure and contrite heart and spirit, and pledge allegiance to our Heavenly Home, Holy Mount Zion, our Army led**

---

[19]   Readers Digest, <u>Mysteries of the Bible</u>, (1998), pg. 134

by Jesus Christ, Majestic Conquering Lion of Judah, the Instructions, Utterances, and Groanings of the Holy Spirit, and Almighty God, Master of the Universe, our Eternal Father. Selah.

"If the world hate you, ye know that it hated Me before it hated you. If ye were of the world, the world would love his own: but because ye are not of the world, but I have chosen you out of the world, therefore the world hateth you."

(John 15: 18, 19)

"I have given them Thy word; and the world hath hated them, because they are not of the world, even as I am not of the world."

(John 17: 14)

"Ye are of God, little children, and have overcome them: because greater is He that is in you, than he that is in the world."

(1 John 4:4)

"And He said unto them, go ye into all the world, and preach the gospel to every creature."

(Mark 16: 15)

NONE OF THESE PHARISEES

"And He taught, saying unto them, is it not written, My
house shall be called of all nations the house of prayer? But ye
have made it a den of thieves."
(Mark 11: 17)

**"Let no man tell you what your personal relationship is with the
Father, (Son, and Holy Ghost). Each man must seek out the Father
for himself, and in fear and trembling."** This was taught to me when I
was very young, by the late Thomas Anderson, my earthly father. (Thank
you daddy!). He also taught me to watch out for cults, and churches that
practice cult like teachings. This proved to be the most important, and
soul saving information that any one could receive.

"For we have not followed cunningly devised fables, when we
made known unto you the Power and Coming of our Lord
Jesus Christ, but were eye witnesses of His Majesty."
(2 Peter 1: 16)

**The world is so full of worldly religions, doctrines, ceremonies,
rituals, church hierarchies and spiritually unrelated activities, that
one could become very confused and inadvertently follow a system**

that would lead them straight to the pits of hell. These systems are so full of apostasy, idolatry, meaningless and spiritually dead rituals, feigning Spirituality, insincerity, trickery, and void of the True Word of God, Jesus, as the Majestic Conquering Lion of Judah (not *only* as the lamb of God!); and the movement of the Holy Spirit, to guide, direct, convict, reprove, comfort, purify, protect and impart spiritual gifts. Let us explore the historical accounts of religious organizations.

The spirit of apostasy, by which the church had become so permeated, before Constantine threw about it the mantle of imperial protection and emblazoned it with insignia of state, now was roused to increased activity, as the leaven of satan's own culture flourished under the conditions most favorable for such fungoid growth. The bishop of Rome had already asserted supremacy over his fellows in the episcopate; but when the emperor made Byzantium his capital and renamed it in his own honor, Constantinople, the bishop of that city claimed equality with the Roman pontiff. The claim was contested; the ensuing dissension divided the church; and the disruption has persisted until the present day, as is evidenced by the existing distinction between the Roman Catholic, and the Greek Catholic churches. The Roman pontiff exercised secular as well as spiritual authority; and in the eleventh century arrogated to himself the title of pope, signifying father, in the sense of paternal ruler in all things. During the twelfth and thirteenth centuries, the temporal authority of the pope was superior to that of kings and emperors; and the Roman church became the despotic potentate of nations, and an autocrat above all secular states. Yet this church, reeking with the stench of worldly ambition and lust of dominance, audaciously claimed to be the church established by Him Who affirmed: "My Kingdom is not of this world." The arrogant assumptions of the church of Rome were not less extravagant in spiritual than in secular administration. In her loudly asserted control over the spiritual destinies of the souls of men, she blasphemously pretended to forgive or retain individual sins, and to inflict or remit all sorts of covert tortures, and bartered for gold charters of indulgent forgiveness for sins already done. Her pope, proclaiming himself the vicar of God, sat in state to judge as God Himself; and by such blasphemy fulfilled the prophecy of Paul following his warning in relation to the awful conditions antecedent to come, except there come a falling away first, and that man of sin be revealed, the son of perdition; who opposeth and exalteth himself above all that is called God, or that is worshipped; so that he as God sitteth in the temple of God, shewing himself that he is God." **In her unrestrained abandon to the license of arrogant authority, the church of rome hesitated not to transgress the law of God, change the ordinances essential to salvation, and ruthlessly break the everlasting covenant, thereby defiling the earth even as Isaiah had foretold.** She altered the ordinance of baptism, destroying its symbolism and associating with it imitations of pagan rites; she corrupted the Sacrament of the Lord's Supper and befouled the doctrine thereof by the vagary of transubstantiation (the roman catholic and eastern orthodox doctrine that the bread and wine of Communion become in substance, but not in appearance, the body and blood of Jesus Christ at consecration); she assumed to apply the merits of the righteous to the forgiveness of the sinner in the unscriptural and wholly repellent dogma of supererogation (the performance of work beyond what is required or expected); she promoted idolatry in most seductive and pernicious forms; she penalized the study of the Holy Scriptures by the people at large; she enjoined an unnatural state of celibacy upon her clergy; she reveled in unholy union with the theories and sophistries of men; and so adulterated the simple doctrines of the Gospel of Christ as to produce a creed rank with superstition and heresy; she promulgated and perverted doctrines regarding the human body as to make the divinely formed tabernacle of flesh appear as a thing fit only to be tortured and condemned; she proclaimed it an act of virtue insuring rich reward to lie and deceive if thereby her own interests might be subserved; and she so thoroughly departed from the original plan of church organization as to make of herself a spectacle or ornate display fabricated by the caprice of man. The most important of the internal causes by which the apostasy of the primitive church was brought about may be thus summarized: (1) The corrupting of the simple doctrines of the Gospel of Christ by admixture with so called philosophic systems. (2) Unauthorized additions to the prescribed rites of the church and the introduction of vital alterations in essential ordinances. (3) Unauthorized changes in church organization and government. Under the tyrannous repression incident to usurped and unrighteous domination by the roman church, civilization was retarded and for centuries was practically halted in its course. The period of retrogression is known in history as the Dark Ages. The fifteenth century witnessed the movement known as the Renaissance or Revival of Learning; there was a general and significantly rapid awakening among men, and a determined effort to shake off the stupor of indolence and ignorance was manifest throughout the civilized world. By historians and philosophers the revival has been regarded as an unconscious and spontaneous prompting of the "spirit of the times;" it was a development predetermined in the Mind of God to illumine the benighted minds of men in preparation for the restoration of the Gospel of Jesus Christ, which was appointed to be accomplished some centuries later. A notable revolt against the papacy occurred in the sixteenth century, and is known as the Reformation. This movement was begun in 1517 by Martin Luther, a German monk; and it spread so rapidly as soon to involve the whole domain of popedom. Formal protests against the despotism of the papal church were formulated by the representatives of certain German principalities and other delegates at a diet or general council held at Spires A.D. 1529; and the reformers were thenceforth known as protestants. An independent church was proposed by John, Elector of Saxony, constitution for which was prepared at his instance by Luther and his colleague, Melanchthon. The protestants were discordant. Being devoid of divine authority to guide them in matters of church organization and doctrine, they followed the diverse ways of men, and were rent within while assailed from without. The roman church, confronted by determined opponents, hesitated at no extreme of cruelty. The court of the inquisition, which had been established in the latter part of the fifteenth century under the infamously sacrilegious name of the "holy office", became intoxicated with the lust of barbarous cruelty in the century of the reformation and inflicted indescribable tortures on persons secretly accused of heresy. In the early stages of the reformation instigated by Luther, the king of england, henry VIII, declared himself a supporter of the pope, and was rewarded by a papal bestowal of the distinguishing title "defender of the faith". Within a few years, this same british sovereign was excommunicated from the roman church, because of impatient disregard of the pope's authority in the matter of henry's desire to divorce Queen Catherine so that he could marry one of her maids. The british parliament, in 1534, passed the act of supremacy, by which the nation was declared free from all allegiance to papal authority. By an act of parliament the king was made the head of the church within his own dominions. Thus was born the church of england, a direct result of the licentious amours of a debauched and infamous king. With blasphemous indifference to the absence of Divine commission, with no semblance of priestly succession, an adulterous sovereign created a church, provided therein a "priesthood" of his own, and proclaimed himself supreme administrator in all matters spiritual. With the conflict between catholicism and protestantism in great britain the student of history is familiar. Suffice it here to say that the mutual hatred of the two contending sects, the zeal of their respective adherents, their professed love of God and devotion to Christ's service, were chiefly signalized by the sword, the ax, and the stake. Reveling in a realization of at least a partial emancipation from the tyranny of priest craft, men and nations debauched their newly acquired liberty of thought, speech, and action, in a riot of abhorrent excess. The mis-called age of reason, and the atheistically abominations culminating in the french revolution stand as ineffaceable testimony of what man may become when glorying in his denial of God. Is it to be wondered at, that from the sixteenth century onward, churches of man's contriving have multiplied with phenomenal rapidity? Churches and churchly organizations professing Christianity as their creed have come to be numbered by hundreds. On every side is heard in this day, "Lo, here is Christ" or "Lo there." There are sects named from the circumstances of their origin—as the church of england; others after their famous founders or promoters—as lutheran, calvinist, wesleyan; some are known by peculiarities of doctrine or plan of administration—as methodist, presbyterian, baptist, congregationalist; but down to the third decade of the nineteenth century there was no church on earth affirming name or title as the Church of Jesus Christ. The only organization called a church existing at that time and venturing to assert claim to authority by succession was the catholic church, which for centuries had been apostate and wholly bereft of Divine authority or recognition.[20]

".... Also he observed times, and used enchantments, and used witchcraft, and dealt with a familiar spirit, and with wizards: he wrought much evil in the sight of the Lord, to provoke Him to anger."

(2 Chronicles 33:6)

---

[20]   Talmage, James E., <u>Jesus The Christ</u>, (1981), pgs 746-749

If the "mother church" be without a valid priesthood, and devoid of Spiritual power, how can her offspring derive from her, the right to officiate in the things of God? Who would dare to affirm that man can originate a priesthood which God is bound to honor and acknowledge? Granted that men may, and do create among themselves secret societies, associations, sects, and even "churches" if they so choose to designate their organization; granted that they may prescribe rules, formulate laws, implement ceremonies and rituals, and devise plans of operation, discipline, and government, and that all such laws, rules, and schemes of administration are binding upon those who assume membership. How can such vain and defective human institutions derive the authority of the Holy Priesthood, without which there can be no Church of Christ? The apostate condition of Christendom has been frankly admitted by many eminent and conscientious representatives of the several churches, and by churches as institutions. Even the Church of England acknowledges the awful fact in her official declaration of degeneracy, as set forth in the "Homily Against which there can be no Church of Christ?

The apostate condition of Christendom has been frankly admitted by many eminent and conscientious representatives of the several churches, and by churches as institutions. Even the church of england acknowledges the awful fact in her official declaration of degeneracy, as set forth in the "homily against peril of idolatry," in these words: "So that laity and clergy, learned and unlearned, all ages, sects, and degrees of men, women, and children of whole Christendom—an horrible and most dreadful thing to think—have been at once drowned in abominable idolatry; of all other vices most detested of God, and most damnable to man; and that by the space of eight hundred years and more."[21]

(Throughout history) one of the most definitive goals of the illuminati (conspiratorial organization which controls world affairs through government and corporations) was to destroy all religions, including Christianity. It may seem to be a contradiction to state that communism and catholicism and protestantism will unite under one banner (and) wants to destroy Christianity. However, communism is not being run by

---

[21] Crouch, Paul, <u>The Shadow of the Apocalypse</u>, (1995), pgs. 49-63

communists, but by the luciferians, who control the wealth of the world. They want to cause another "reign of terror," and this time the anarchy is to be world-wide. Communism, catholicism, and protestantism are ALL just tools of the devil which he is using to eventually destroy the *Real Religion of the Bible,* and attempt to make lucifer the only god of this world. Using catholicism, protestantism, and communism, the luciferians hope to throw the world into complete mayhem, so in the end, the people of the world who survive this coming holocaust will become disillusioned with both Christianity and communism, and just as during the french revolution, blame Christianity and Christ as the reasons for the worlds problems. This is no nursery rhyme or part in a play we have been presenting before you, these things are for real, and deadly serious. This is satan's last effort to take complete control of this world.[22]

> "He that turneth away his ear from hearing the law, even his prayer shall be abomination. Whoso causeth the righteous to go astray in an evil way, he shall fall himself into his own pit: but the upright shall have good things in his possession.
> (Proverbs 28: 9, 10)

The history of the roman catholic church, dark, ominous and very disturbing; and most of the denominations that have come out of her, are disturbing as well, considering the derangement, and spiritual darkness of the "mother." Biblical text states the sins of the fathers will fall upon the children down to the fourth and fifth generations. One must wonder if this extends to "church fathers and mothers", as well as that of family. It seems so! Is it no wonder that most churches are heaped with imperfections and much nonsense—hollow rituals, doctrines of men, excommunications, spiritual tyranny, political and spiritual adultery, and the absence of the Holy Ghost? Is it no wonder that mankind is perplexed and stupefied wondering which is the true faith to follow?

---

[22]   Anderson, Roy Allen, <u>The illuminati 666</u>, (1983), pgs. 252, 253

"Know ye not that ye are the temple of God, and that the Spirit of God dwelleth in you? If any man defile the temple of God, him shall God destroy; for the temple of God is Holy, which temple ye are. Let no man deceive himself. If any man among you seemeth to be wise in this world, let him become a fool, that he may be wise. For the wisdom of this world is foolishness with God. For it is written, He taketh the wise in their own craftiness. And again, The Lord knoweth the thoughts of the wise, that they are vain. Therefore let no man glory in men. For all things are yours; whether Paul, or Apollos, or Cephas, or the world, or life, or death, or things present, or things to come; all are yours; and ye are Christ's; and Christ is God's.

(1 Corinthians 3:16-23)

In the Book of Revelations John is given a message from Jesus concerning seven letters to seven churches of the time. In these letters, He gives positive or negative feedback according to what has been earned. The letters are addressed to the congregations of the churches at Ephesus, Smyrna, Pergamos, Thyatira, Sardis, Philadelphia, and Laodicea. The concerns that Jesus addresses are the same concerns present in today's churches. To fully understand the significance of these seven letters, we need to capture the intent, which was Jesus providing information to meet His expectations:

Literal—The reprimand in each letter was intended to be applied immediately to the very real problem being faced by the actual church to which the letter was addressed.

Symbolic—Because the issues raised in each letter are universal issues faced by every church, the seven churches in Revelations can be viewed as symbolic of all churches throughout history.

Personal—Because these seven messages were also given to any individual "who has an ear to hear", we know they have something of significance to say to you and me!

Historic—If you examine, in order, the challenges outlined in each of the seven letters, you will find that they address the same problems and phases that have characterized the chronology of the church over the past two thousand years—and in the same order![23]

Let us see what Jesus had to say to each church:

Ephesus (the loveless church) means "my darling, my desired one." Jesus said "Nevertheless I have somewhat against thee, because thou hast left thy first love." Despite all their excellent programs and efforts, they had departed from their early heartfelt affection for the Lord! To leave a first love is the first step toward a great fall. The Judge entreats them to repent, change their attitude, and return to their first love by doing the things they had done in the beginning.

Smyrna (the persecuted church) was often called the "glory of Asia". Christ commends the church for remaining true to the Word of God. He offers no rebuke to the church at Smyrna. Presenting Himself as One Who has already conquered death and will never die again, Jesus acknowledges their suffering, affliction, and poverty for the sake of His name. Christ promises that the overcomer, even if he suffers physical death, will not suffer the "second death," another phrase for eternal death, or spending eternity in the lake of fire and separated from God.

Pergamos (the worldly church) means "mixed marriage," a perverted marriage, or a commingling with the world. The Book of Revelation refers to Pergamos as a place "where satan has his throne" and "where satan lives". Christ commends the church for remaining true to the Word of God. Nevertheless, there were those in the church who embraced the doctrine of Balaam and the Nicolaitans, denying the deity of Christ. Many had also been lured into sexual immorality and intermarrying with idolater, thereby weakening their Christian resolve. The message to the Christians at Pergamos is to repent and return to the Word of God or face the double-edged sword of Christ's mouth, symbolizing the Word of God.

---

[23]   Crouch, Paul, <u>The Shadow of the Apocalypse</u>, (1995), pgs. 49-56

Thyatira (the paganized church) mean "continual sacrifice", and indeed, this name is fitting for a church that still engaged in making sacrifices to idols and thus discounting Christ's work on the cross, which provided the final sacrifice—payment in full—for all of our sins. Christ commends the church for its charity, service, good works and faith, but again He delivers His criticism, charging the church with tolerating the teachings of the false prophetess Jezebel, Ahab's evil consort who introduced phoenician cults to Israel in First and Second Kings. Thyatira had tolerated false teachings leading to sexual immorality (a symbol of idolatry) as well as the eating of food sacrificed to idols (symbolizing a union of the church with the world). Christ declares that He had given ample opportunity for the church to repent, yet they had not. Then, He declares that He will cast them into great tribulation unless they repent. Christ promises that those who overcome these influences will participate in the leadership of His kingdom and He will give them the morning star, a reference to His presence in their lives.

Sardis (the lifeless church) means "remnant" and indeed, in this letter Jesus appears to be calling a remnant of believers out of a spiritually dead environment and into a renewed relationship with him. Christ's commendation of this church is the shortest of all the churches. Christ says the congregation at Sardis, was nothing short of spiritually dead. Apparently their focus had evolved from enjoying a personal relationship with Christ to pleasing political leaders. They had substituted formal pageantry and ornate ritualism for true worship, and they trusted in the state rather than in God to meet their needs in times of economic hardship. The church at Sardis was also guilty of nominal Christianity, accepting members into the church without encouraging or requiring any kind of spiritual renewal. The Lord calls upon this church to (1) wake up, (2) strengthen what remains, (3) remember what it has received and heard (God's Word), (4) keep God's word and (5) repent. Christ warns that failure to do this will result in judgment instead of blessing at the Lord's return. He cautions them that if they do not repent, He will come as a thief. They will be caught by surprise at His second coming, and their names will be erased from the book of life. Christ promises any overcomers that they will be clothed in white raiment, that their names will not be removed from the book of life, and that He will confess them before His Father.

Philadelphia (the missionary church) means "brotherly love". Christ offers no rebuke to the Christians at Philadelphia—only commendation, because they have kept the word of His patience. Christ promises that He will make heretics worship at their feet and know that He has loved them. He also promises that this church will be spared the horror of the Tribulation period. This promise applies to all Christians who have kept His commandments and endured patiently. He promises to return for His own, and He promises rewards for Christians who overcome. In this letter, believers are clearly identified as God's own possessions and the inhabitants of the New Jerusalem. To those who overcome, Jesus says; they will be as pillars in the Temple of God, and He will write on them His new name!

Laodicea (the lukewarm church) had nothing for which Christ could commend it. Actually the best He can say is that they are "neither cold nor hot"—lukewarm. This church thought of itself as rich and in need of nothing. It focused on social propriety and materialism. It may have been involved in a building program or market research or elaborate social events to please its parishioners and make Christianity palatable to the community, but Christ labels it wretched, miserable, poor, blind and naked. The letter describes Christ standing outside the door, knocking. This disturbing indictment against the church of Laodicea echoes a wake-up call to Christians today. Christ invites us to hear His voice, to open the door, and to invite Him in. If we do, He promises to come in and commune with us. Today, Jesus still stands, knocking at the door of human hearts, waiting to be invited in. Finally, Jesus promises all overcomers that they will be granted a seat with Christ on His throne.[24]

In these letters exist a vivid portrayal of the expectations, constructive criticism, and promises that Jesus has for first century Christians, and for church leaders and congregations of today. Regardless of where we are as a church, parishioner, or clergy, Christ's message is one of hope, correction,

---

[24] Crouch, Paul, The Shadow of the Apocalypse, (1995), pgs. 56-63

and possibility to enter the Eternal Kingdom. Jesus is calling us to repent, if any of our modern day churches fall into any of the five churches that He had to correct. Jesus is beseeching that we fall back in love with Him, pledge allegiance to Him, to fear not, even in the face of persecution, and especially to stop committing spiritual adultery. Be like the churches of Philadelphia and Smyrna! Be aware, be strong, be rich in Him, be zealous and militant, and be clothed in His righteousness, and open the door speedily when He knocks.

The history of the chaos of the churches, sadly persist even today, and more prevalently. Some denominations continue to encourage idolatry, payment for prayers and to forgive sin, celibacy, nuns who believe *they* are the bride of Christ, secret societies, "first ladies", homosexual choir directors—twisting and gyrating on the pulpit—(Is this God's choice to lead His people in high praise!?), "puffedupness", meaningless "church hierarchies", feigned "good works" for the benefit of the leader, servitude to the leaders and "first ladies", perversion of the sacrament, activities that pad the pockets of the pastor and not the storehouse (**high treason!!!**), sexual immorality, homosexuality, lesbianism, and the sensationalism of the choir and pastor, sadly identified and mistaken as the Holy Spirit. *If you cannot feel the move of the Holy Spirit during your quiet prayer, reflection, and meditation, then what you're feeling during the song, dance, and preaching of the pastor, is most often not the Holy Spirit.* It is merely a release of endorphins in the brain (the feel good hormones). Others teach only what they believe their followers want to hear, for fear of dwindling their congregations and their financial intake. Most are concerned with the monetary value of their books, their tapes, and the tithes of the followers, using scripture, often out of context for monetary gain, and reciting scriptures over and over (brainwashing) for increased economic gain, and "sleeping" with politicians to provide congregational votes in exchange for monetary gain and political clout. These, of course, keep them in the bountiful lifestyles to which they have become accustomed. Still, others are consumed with stealing God's glory, claiming to be the spokesperson for God on earth (without proper authority), or claiming to be God on earth, bullying, oppressing, committing spiritual tyranny, spiritual adultery, and the debauchery continues to grow, with ever increasing gusto! All proclaim a certain disciplinary adherence to their particular brand of doctrines, laws, policies, and church hierarchy, but are they the doctrines, laws, policies, and church hierarchy of God Almighty? Most definitely not!!! Most are comprised of persons who could not make it in the world; so they now run to the church for some position, or title, or self aggrandizement. How can you find God in the midst of all this evil, grandiose, selfish, and self serving foolishness!?

"It is better to trust in the Lord than to put confidence in man. It is better to trust in the Lord than to put confidence in princes."

(Psalm 118: 8, 9)

"We know that we have passed from death unto life, because we love the brethren. He that loveth not his brother abideth in death. Whosoever hateth his brother is a murderer: and ye know that no murderer hath eternal life abiding in him. Hereby perceive we the love of God, because He laid down his life for us: and we ought to lay down our life for the brethren. But whoso hath this world's good, and seeth his brother have need, and shutteth up his bowels of compassion from him, how dwelleth the love of God in him? My little children, let us not love in word, neither in tongue but in deed and in truth. And hereby we know that we are of the truth, and shall assure our hearts before Him."

(1 John 3: 14-19)

Just because a church is not called the church of satan, does not mean it is not a church where satan has supreme control. It seems satan was alive and very well at the churches of Sardis, Pergamos, Thyatira, Laodecia, and Ephesus; and satan presides over most of the churches today, to try to deceive, even the elect with all types of "churchly" distractions and untruths. The one world religion spoken of in the Book of Revelations, has been in existence for centuries. These "split offs" from roman catholicism are too distracted with apologetics, and church "business", to be able to impart a word of truth (that they themselves have no clue of), or the agenda for these last days, and they all fall under the umbrella of their deranged mother, the roman catholic church—many churches, one mother, and all concerned with wealth accumulation! The leaders of these churches will boldly tell you the "church" is a business. Whose business!? Certainly not God's! Be wise and don't be misguided by the wiles of the devil, he enters many churches in various disguises, with nonsensical agendas, rituals, and with exactly what pleases us most. He is running things in a lot of these churches!!

Some say it matters not what church you go to as long as you go to church. Be careful, the devil is operational in many churches. His agenda is not about getting you to a place where your walk with God is in servitude, righteousness, and doing God's will. It is quite the opposite. The enemy provides you with a false sense of Godliness, which is powerless, fruitless, and hell bound! Your pleasure must stay in the Father's truth—the Word of God, the Testimony of Jesus, and the Guidance of the Holy Spirit. You must trust the Voice of the Spirit, and never doubt, He will always surely work it out!!

> "He that oppresseth the poor to increase his riches, and he that giveth to the rich shall surely come to want."
> (Proverbs 22:16)

> "A true witness delivereth souls: but a deceitful witness speaketh lies."
> (Proverbs 14: 25)

> "Lying lips are abomination to the Lord: but they that deal truly are His delight."
> (Proverbs 12: 22)

> "Woe be unto the pastors that destroy and scatter the sheep of My pasture! Saith the Lord. Therefore thus saith the Lord God of Israel against the pastors that feed My people; ye have scattered My flock, and driven them away, and have not visited

them: behold, I will visit upon you the evil of your doings,
saith the Lord.

(Jeremiah 23: 1.2)

Which of these seven churches do you pastor or attend? Hopefully
Philadelphia and/or Smyrna! This requires very attentive spiritual scrutiny.
Your very soul salvation and the salvation of your congregation is at stake!
Especially you pastors, bishops, preachers, teachers, and counselors, God
has entrusted His people into your hands; His people that He loves so
very much! If error is found in your ministry, or your walk, make haste
to change it, repent, and commence to do the *real and true* Will of our
Father. We must take responsibility for our own spiritual evolvement, as
well as those God has placed in our hands. This must always be done in
righteousness and truth under the protection and guidance of the Holy
Spirit.

> "And though they say, The Lord liveth; surely they swear falsely.
> O Lord, are not thine eyes upon the truth? Thou has stricken
> them, but they have not grieved; thou hast consumed them, but
> they have refused to receive correction: they have made their
> faces harder than a rock; they have refused to return. Therefore
> I said, surely these are poor; they are foolish: for they know not
> the way of the Lord, nor the judgment of their God."
>
> (Jeremiah 5: 2-4)

As far as churches are concerned, most are full of thievery and trickery; they
all fall short of the Glory of the Father, the Word of God, the Priesthood
set up by Jesus Christ, and the *true* move of the Holy Spirit. The leaders
and congregations are not giving Him obedient love, not loving their
brothers and sisters, and especially and above all—**NOT SHARING
THE TITHES IN THE STOREHOUSE—HIGH TREASON!!!** The
tithes are not for the pastor to live an opulent lifestyle. It was meant for

the widows and orphans, and those in great need, like in such a time as this!! Faithful tithers of these churches, some who have tithed for decades, cannot receive a dime when they are in need! That is so wickedly wrong, and our Father in heaven is fed up with the use, abuse, and the robbing of His people without a gun! These "pastors" are actually pimping God!!! Until the tithes are distributed as God intended, we should not get caught up in this new "hustle;" and trying to decide if we should pay our "tithe" or pay the mortgage. We wonder, as we tithe into these "churches", for decades, why God has not poured down a blessing that we have not room enough to receive (Malachi 3: 10). The answer is quite simple. **We are not tithing in good ground as He instructed us to do, and we are casting our pearls before swine, as He instructed us not to do!** We know God does not lie, neither does His Word return to Him void. *It is what we're doing wrong*; being blind, misled, super stupid, and putting our faith in a man with a few shiny trinkets, and not in God!!

As we enter into any church denomination, we must be ever vigilantly in tuned with the Holy Spirit to receive His gift of discernment, so that we may recognize Who the Holy Spirit really is, and not mistake Him for the music, the dance, and the sensationalism and charisma of the choir and/or the pastor. These do not make a true, Spirit filled church. A church cannot demonstrate perfection unless the Holy Ghost resides there! And, as we know, the Holy Ghost will not dwell in an unclean temple!

"For the Lord God will help me; therefore shall I not be confounded."

(Isaiah 50:7)

"Howbeit the Most High dwelleth not in temples made with hands; as saith the prophet, Heaven is My Throne, and the earth is my footstool: what house will ye build Me? Saith the Lord: or what is the place of My rest? Hath not My Hand made all these things? Ye stiffnecked and uncircumcised in heart and ears, ye do always resist the Holy Ghost: as your fathers did, so do ye. Which of the prophets have not your fathers persecuted? And they have slain them which shewed before of the coming of the Just One; of whom ye have been now the betrayers and murderers: Who have received the law by the disposition of angels, and have not kept it."

(Acts 7: 48-53)

"He that tillith his land shall have plenty of bread: but he that followeth after vain persons shall have poverty enough. A faithful man shall abound with blessings: but he that maketh haste to be rich shall not be innocent."

(Proverbs 28: 19, 20)

TALKING THE TALK

"...This is My Beloved Son: hear Him."
(Mark 9:7)

There are several Christian doctrines derived from the scriptures, Christian doctrines, Christian tradition, and the reflections of Christians today, which bear directly on the role of communication in society. The most important are: creation and stewardship; sin and redemption; the newness of life; good news and proclamation; Christian witness; helping those less fortunate and preparing for the day that Jesus returns to earth for battle.

God the creator of all things visible and invisible is a central Christian doctrine. This means that all things are interrelated, that the eternal order of things is revealed in historical order, and that we human beings are not the creators, but rather are bound together as part of creation, along with all other parts of creation, in affinity. This concept, in and of itself, should be humbling, and make us want to strive to ensure the safety, security, and comfort of others, because we are all family—interconnected.

Creation includes the techniques of social communication—the telephone, radio, television, movies, newspapers, internet and so on. Without these technologies, humankind simply would be unable to live in the complex social structures we now enjoy or hate. Since all elements of social communication are first of all God's creation, and not our creation, they must be thought of as being held in trust by those who use them.

Stewardship is a necessary outcome of creation. The mass media are an especially powerful and most times evil force in society, censoring and distorting news and events as they are often instructed to, by the powers that be. The importance of exercising stewardship in the use of them for good, is a misnomer because the Holy Spirit will not utilize a less than righteous tool. Mass media, for the most part, is controlled and exploited by the evil ones, therefore, what of it can be believed, fully? All things related to mass media are preplanned and orchestrated, so there can be no Supernatural move of the Spirit. Within it exists brainwashing, conditioning, and fear mongering. The Spirit will have no part with this.

Evil is not created by God. Because it exists only in potential until actualized by human choice, evil serves as a decision stimulus the moral progress of free-will human beings. Free will is an attribute bestowed by God on his mortal children to enable them to choose between good and evil, and to ascend from imperfection to perfection. The Creator will not allow any being to deny you the right to exercise your divinely bestowed free will. We are all part of a gigantic creation striving towards perfection, and perfection only exists where God exists. Evil is the immature choosing and the unthinking misstep of those who are resistant to goodness, rejectful of beauty, and disloyal to truth. [25]

The Biblical record and Christian traditions are clear that human beings are expected by their Creator to use the good things of the earth to accomplish God's will: the building of a just, peaceful, and loving world community. The media of social communication has no potential for aiding in this goal, and uses these techniques purely for profit, self aggrandizement, and mind control over the masses. This is completely ruled out by the Christian understanding of creation and stewardship, and exists outside of the plan of God. This, of course, is sin, and on a very grand scale!

---

[25] TheoQuest.com, <u>The Quest for God is Everything</u>, (2002), pg. 5

"Who is on the Lord's side? Let him come unto Me."
(Exodus 32:26)

Christians understand sin as the misuse of God's gifts. Sin is taking something that is a gift of God—things, money, power, prestige (perks)—and treating it as if it were a god; and selfishly keeping it all to oneself. Sin is not something that people are simply thrust into by events, but is the result of deliberate choice, a choice not to live up to God's expectations for the full potential of all human beings, but rather to further the self at the expense of others. The very rich and politically powerful constantly misuse the God given power over creation. Instead of using their "gifts" to bring about harmony, peace, love, and security in all creation and its interrelatedness, they misuse this power for selfish purposes. Why? Because God is not the benefactor of their "gifts." Their power comes from the evil one.

"Hell and destruction are never full; so the eyes of man are never satisfied."
(Proverbs 27: 20)

Christian doctrine takes seriously the concept that God makes all things new, that novelty and creativity are essential elements of God's world. Therefore, Christians resist any attempts to restrict or alter communication, and the release of information, so that persons are not restricted and oppressed in their choices. New ideas, new values, and new understanding are essential to growth, to human potentiality, and an increase in Spiritual knowledge. There are those who do not promote this on any level, especially not Spiritually. Any policy or regulation which would restrict opportunities for a person to grow in knowledge, is sin, since it allows one person or group to dominate and regulate the informational intake of others, molding them into some sort of mindless puppet. Christian belief insists on remaining open to the Spirit, and rejects attempts to restrain

the way the Spirit delivers information. It also rejects one sided flows of communication. It is understood, that God works in mysterious ways, and can never be fully understood, or predicted. The good news requires that communication in the community takes into account all persons, and the whole person; and that it deals with them as sons and daughters of God, allowing the Holy Spirit to deal with each of them on a very personal (and individual level.) Communication that does otherwise, that treats persons as objects, is in fact oppressing them, this is totalitarianism. Finally, Christian doctrine challenges falsehood. Christianity is not "evenhanded." It has a bias toward what it perceives to be real and true. The fact that we live in a pluralistic society means that as Christians we must be a witness for the truth as we perceive it while at the same time being open to hear the truth as perceived by others.[26]

Communication is the exchange of information between people by means of speaking, writing, or using a common system of signs, behavior, body language, and eye contact. It is also a sense of mutual understanding and empathy. Behavior and body language must always be congruent with what is being communicated. For example we cannot and should never feign empathy by using kind words, yet having a scowl on our face, and exhibiting pompous behavior. It is not always what you say, but how you say it. Insincere responses will disable the Holy Spirit's action in guiding us to give the recipient the needed information. We must also be culturally sensitive since we exist in a multicultural society. Those in the teaching, preaching, and counseling professions would do well to take a cultural sensitivity course, or invest in some cultural sensitivity books. Wherever we go, whom ever we communicate with, we should be able to communicate effectively, efficiently, and with a high level of sensitivity and decorum. We must exhibit the persona of Jesus in all of our exchanges. Can you *walk* the *talk*!?

In all walks of life, communication is essential in dealing with people in casual, professional, and/or theological arenas. Candor and kindness is very important, however when difficult discussions are necessary, it is important to be able to communicate without being condescending,

---

[26]   www.bibleknowledge.com

offensive, or appearing disinterested. Sometimes, the recipient may become defensive, or irate, or condescending. It is imperative not to escalate with the person with whom we are communicating. If this happens, you've just lost the opportunity to be of service to that person. Nothing you say from that day and in the future will ever carry any weight, be believed, or be considered valuable. What will be remembered is that you behaved in a totally unprofessional, and inappropriate manner, especially those in leadership.

> "Let him that is taught in the Word communicate unto Him that teacheth in all good things."
> (Galatians 6: 6)

It is alright to sometimes become angry; we would not be human if we never felt this negative human emotion. It is not alright to demonstrate that anger, condescension, or disinterest towards those who are hurting, that we are teaching, preaching, counseling, or just engaging in casual conversation. We must realize that the persons anger toward us is often misplaced. They are not angry with us, only with their situation, the state of the world's economy, and are most definitely not coping very well. We should not take these affronts personally. We must always maintain control of the situation by continuing to speak in a calming, non threatening, and reassuring manner. We may even make a comment such as, "I can understand how this situation must be very difficult and frustrating for you." This demonstrates empathy, and shows that you care about their feelings and circumstances, and that you desire to be instrumental in assisting to resolve the issue. Above all, we must be able to forgive when we feel we've been personally attacked or disrespected. Forgiveness releases you from anger and/or bitterness, which only serves to annihilate your joy. Forgiveness is purifying and gives you the opportunity to actively release all of your negative emotions associated with the affront, keep your joy, and return to the business of helping to resolve problems. We always want to extend the love of Jesus in everything we say. It is difficult to demonstrate the likeness of Jesus with persons who are very difficult to

deal with, especially those that are negativistic, angry, or bitter most of the time. Just remember how loving and forgiving our Father is despite our own indiscretions, and demonstrate this in like. Some of these people have not known pure love and concern. Rely on the Holy Spirit for patience, calmness of spirit, the right words of comfort, and helpful resolutions. The more you practice being in servitude to those in need, the more we please our Father and the more rewarding it becomes.

> "But love ye your enemies, and do good, and lend hoping for nothing again; and your reward shall be great, and ye shall be the children of the Highest; for He is kind unto the unthankful and to the evil. Be ye therefore merciful, as your Father also is merciful. Judge not, and ye shall not be judged: condemn not, and ye shall not be condemned: forgive, and ye shall be forgiven: Give, and it shall be given unto you; good measure, pressed down, and shaken together, and running over, shall men give into your bosom. For with the same measure that ye mete withal it shall be measured to you again."
> (Luke 6: 35-38)

In today's world most people are tense, preoccupied, angry, bitter, frightened and unhappy. It's the trickle down effect of the world's failing economy, the failure and impotence of the so called—world leaders, church leaders, and the absence of faith among the masses. People are losing jobs, homes, being demoted in their rate of pay, and as a result, there is increased tension in the home—leading to disagreements, arguments, physical fighting, and even divorce. Add to this the children who cannot be given the worldly things that they are used to receiving, and may be acting out as a result. It is especially important, now more than ever, to be especially patient, kind, and caring.

These acts must be demonstrated with sincerity of heart. People know when you are feigning emotions that you really don't feel, or pretending to care when you really don't; as a result you will lose all credibility and the opportunity to serve them. With all the negativity that is happening in the world around us, more people will seek their clergy, or family members for answers. We will remind them that all that is happening is fulfillment of the prophetic Book of Revelations. All these things must come to pass because God's Word will never return to Him void. Remind them of what it is to be a faithful overcomer, and the promises and rewards from God when we are faithful to the end. Remind them that all these negative events were foretold, and are a clear indication of Jesus' imminent return. Jesus said it would not be easy, but it would be worth it. We should look at these events as necessary, welcome them, and know that His Kingdom come, and very, very soon! Remind them to stay fixed on Him, and not only on their situations. Remind them that when Jesus comes down in a cloud of glory, He is coming to do battle, and then take us home where there are no more tears, anxiety, sickness, and suffering. Remind them that it is our job to endure until the end. During our period of endurance, trials, and suffering, we must continue to give Him thanks and praise. Hallelujah Anyhow!!!! Our circumstances could have always been so much worse!

> "Sing unto the Lord, O ye saints of His, and give thanks at the remembrance of His Holiness. For His anger endureth but a moment; in His favour is life: weeping may endure for a night, but joy cometh in the morning."
> (Psalms 30" 4-5)

Communication also involves active listening. You are not listening if you're thinking of what you're going to say next. We must permit the person with whom we are communicating with to complete their thoughts and sentences. Then wait a moment before responding, listening for the utterances of the Holy Spirit. Let us not try to resolve issues on our own. This is vanity and could compound the problem. We must wait for the move of the Spirit Who is able to transform any situation. When people are seeking assistance, they are looking for real and tangible solutions. They do not want, nor will they appreciate being placated—pleasant talk with no substantiation. If there are no immediate solutions, you can always tell them that you will pray over the matter, find out what answers the Holy Spirit will impart, and get back to them; and that they should also do the same, He will speak to them, as well as us. It is imperative that you follow up as promised or you risk losing all credibility.

> "He that speaketh truth sheweth forth righteousness: but a false witness deceit."
> (Proverbs 12:17)

We never want to acquire a reputation of not being reliable, not making good on our word, or providing misinformation. This is exactly why we must pray and listen for the guidance of the Holy Spirit. His answers, decisions, and corrections are always perfect in every way. He has all the answers! We, of our finite selves, do not.

> "As for God, His way is perfect: the Word of the Lord is tried: He is a buckler to all those that trust in Him. For Who is God that girdeth me with strength, and maketh my way perfect."
> (Psalm 18: 30-32)

We of ourselves only know how to make temporary solutions, often erroneous, in temporary situations. We are not the Omniscient One and only have intellect, and a tiny degree of knowledge; so in communicating with others in any arena, we must practice active listening, administer comfort, offer solutions under the guidance of the Spirit, and we must demonstrate the mercy, tenderness, and forgiveness (when necessary) of the Father, the gentle, loving patience of Christ, and allow the Holy Spirit to work through us, without interference. Remember, our spirit to His Spirit, is the only way to communicate with Him, in order to intercede for others.

"You are immortal by nature. As spirit soul, you are part of and parcel of Me. I Am Immortal, and so you are also immortal, unnecessarily, you are trying to be happy in this material world."

(Bhagavad-gita 15.7)[27]

"Let your light so shine before men, that they may see your good works and glorify your Father which is in heaven."

(Matthew 5:16)

"And the servant of the Lord must not strive; but be gentle unto all men, apt to teach, patient, in meekness instructing those that oppose themselves; if God peradventure will give them repentance to the acknowledging of the truth; and that they may recover themselves out of the snare of the devil, who are taken captive by him at his will."

(2 Timothy 2:24-26)

"Let love be without dissimulation. Abhor that which is evil; cleave to that which is good. Be kindly affectioned one to another with brotherly love; in honour preferring one another; not slothful in business; fervent in spirit, serving the Lord."

(Romans 12: 9-11)

"Anyone who seriously engages in My service immediately becomes transcendental to the material qualities and comes to the platform of **Brahman**, or Spirit."[28]

---

[27] Bhaktivedanta, A. C., and Prabhapada, Swani, <u>The Journey of Self</u>, (1997), pg.64

[28] Bhaktivedanta, A. C. and Prabhupada, Swami, <u>The Journey of Self Discovery</u>, (1997), pg 9

WALKING THE WALK

"And Enoch walked with God."
(Genesis 5:21)

The apostle Paul said you have to work out your salvation with fear and trembling. Salvation is just the beginning. God has a purpose and plan for each person's life that He wants you to embark on. You are now being given a brand new life with a brand new start. All old things have passed away and all things have now been made truly brand new and wrought with excitement of Spirit. The following are the areas that each new Christian has to be gradually led into if they are really going to enter into the real walk with the Lord:

The Full Surrender—The first thing each Christian has to do after they get saved is to completely surrender their entire life over to God the Father. Jesus has to become Lord over your life, not just your savior. If you want to find out what God's call and plan is going to be for your life, and exactly what He wants to do with your life, then you are going to have to be willing to completely surrender every aspect of your life over to Him. Its your all, for His All. This means to fully surrender everything. You can hold absolutely nothing back. If you do not fully surrender everything over to God, then you prevent Him from working full force in your life. You have to become both saved and surrendered. All Christians are obviously saved, but many are not fully surrendered to the Lord, and that is why very little happens after they initially become saved.

Become Spirit Filled—The next step after a person makes a full surrender to the Father is to become Spirit filled. They need to receive the Baptism of the Holy Spirit operating in your life. You cannot walk this walk without the power of the Holy Spirit operating in your life. It is the Holy Spirit's job to guide you in all that you think, say, or do.

Establish Faith and Trust in God—you must completely surrender your entire life over to Father God and receive the Baptism of the Holy Spirit, the next step is to establish true faith and trust in God. Not the faith you say with your mouth, but the faith that is ever swelling in your heart. The only thing that will bring you into God's realm is faith and belief. Nothing else will. The beautiful thing about this is, God is only looking for a small amount of faith, the size of a mustard seed. The Bible says that faith the size of a mustard seed will move mountains. Your faith will grow, but God does not expect it to grow overnight. All God asks is that you give Him just a little bit to work with, and He will more than prove Himself to you so that you can learn to completely trust Him to guide you on your journey.

Walk in All of God's Ways—The Bible says we now have to learn to walk in all the ways of the Lord, not just some of the ways. The Bible is the number one source where you will learn all the ways of our Father. If you do no learn what His rules and ways are going to be for you in this life, your assignment; then the devil and his demons will come down on you for major attacks and try to take you out. The last thing he wants is for you to live in obedience and walk in the ways of our Father. You must adhere to God's ways if you want to live out your life under His guidance and protection. People's lives are shortened on this earth due to stupidity, and not knowing the ways of God. God said, my people perish for a lack of knowledge.

Obey all of God's Commandments—God also lays out for all of us what He does not want us to do in this life. The bible says that God lays out before each one of us agency, choices on how to live this life. You can either choose God and live this life the way He wants you to live it—or you can choose the enemy and live this life his way, or the world's way, and then end up reaping sorrow, spiritual dysfunction and eventually premature death. There is only one way to live your life and that is God's way, not your way. It really is not your way, but the way of the enemy. God specifically lays out certain sins and transgressions that He wants you to stay away from, the most important is grieving the Holy Spirit, denying Jesus Christ as the Son of God and Redeemer of the world, and being in a never ending state of spiritual stagnation.

(6) **Develop a Personal Relationship With God**—God created mankind for intimate fellowship. He has a special love and longing for mankind and wants more than anything to establish a deep, personal love relationship with each person He has created. Always take the time to love on Him.

(7) **Seek After Knowledge**—God places an extremely high value on the pursuit of Spiritual knowledge. Once you have become saved and born again, God expects you to grow in the knowledge of Him, His Son, His Holy Spirit, and all His ways.

(8) **Establish Relationships With Other Christians**—Once you enter in on this real walk with the Lord, you will need to develop good healthy relationships with other Christians, not just any "Christians", but those who are true to the faith and keep God's statutes. God will start to do some real incredible things in your life. God will lead you to people that He will want you to connect with. You will need other Christians to grow further in the knowledge of God, and to share your walk with them. God will start to do some real incredible things in your life. God will lead you to people that He will want you to connect with. You will need other Christians to grow further in the knowledge of God, and to share your walk with.

Join a Good Spirit Filled Church—Each born again Christian needs to ask The Holy Spirit which church He would like for them to join. There are different levels of the anointing, and sometimes none at all, in all of the different churches. God knows which one would be best suited for your personal Spiritual growth and development in Him. God will make sure that He gets through to each person as to which church He would really like for them to join and become Spiritually active in.

As ministers, teachers, preachers and counselors, we must always lead by example. We can in no way do anything that compromises our integrity. A prime example is, a pastor of a church, teaching about Christian integrity, said, "If it is raining cats and dogs, and I see a woman of the congregation standing at the bus stop, I will not pick her up if my wife is not in the car. Why?" he continued, "This would leave the door open for the enemy to use, for misinterpretation, gossip, and an assault on my character." This may seem over the top, but leaders must always protect themselves from demonic attacks that may attempt to, or actually defile our spiritual walk. This can be a means for contentions, sexual immorality, and other transgressions to enter into the churches. As we know satan and his ministers catch a ride on the back of a backslidden parishioner every worship day in an attempt to destroy ministries. Each pastor needs to pray at the beginning of the service aloud, that if there is anything in the church, that is not of God, leave now in the name of Jesus and by His Most Precious Blood, and return to outer darkness, never to return or to be reassigned! Then open the church door wide to give the evil spirits plenty of room to depart!! Nothing would delight the devil more than to take down a spiritual leader, and destroy his/her ministry.

> "That ye be not soon shaken in mind, or be troubled, neither by spirit, nor by word, nor by letter as from us, as that the day of Christ is at hand. Let no man deceive you by any means: for that day shall not come, except there come a falling away first, and the man of sin be revealed, the son of perdition; who opposeth and exalteth himself above all that is called God, or that is worshipped; so that he sitteth in the temple of God, shewing himself that he is God."
> (2 Thessalonians 2: 2-4)

> "Blessed be the Lord my strength, which teacheth my hands to war, and my fingers to fight: my Goodness, and my Fortress; my High Tower, and my
>
> Deliverer; my Shield, and He in whom I trust; . . . ."
> (Psalms 145: 1, 2)

We must always be vigilantly aware that the devil, as the Bible states, is roaming to and fro seeking whom he may devour. He wants to destroy your mind, he wants to destroy your body, he wants to destroy your career, he wants to destroy your family, he wants to destroy your ministry, and above all, and more than anything, he wants to destroy your anointing. Run in your spirit, into the presence of the Holy Ghost; let Him penetrate your heart, mind, soul, and body, and stay there!!! Stand strong in the Spirit of the Holy Ghost! The devil can't touch that!!!

"Blessed is the man that endureth temptation: for when he is tried, he shall receive the crown of life, which the Lord hath promised to them that love Him. Let no man say when he is tempted, I am tempted of God: for God cannot be tempted with evil, neither tempteth He any man: But every man is tempted, when he is drawn away of his own lust, and enticed. Then when lust hath conceived, it bringeth forth sin: and sin, when it is finished, bringeth forth death. Do not err, my beloved breathren. Every good gift and every perfect gift is from above, and cometh down from the Father of Lights with Whom is no variableness, neither shadow of turning.

(James 1: 12-17)

To walk the Christian walk requires that we not sit casually watching pain, suffering, and those sincerely in need of our assistance, without taking some kind of action. Only the truly surrendered heart is able to discern opportunities, weigh options and take action to demonstrate to others the Greatness, Kindness and Love of Christ. The truly surrendered heart is not a heart of giving up, but a heart willing to fight against darkness and every adversity, even unto the death. How hard you tried does not make any difference if you give up. Opportunities to walk the rough, crooked and narrow road of life, seeking those who truly need our help manifest daily, in these hard days and times of our Lord. However, we are tempted to walk the easy, broad road with others who seem not to have problems, difficulties, and other negative circumstances. We are tempted to walk the easy road where money, influence, things, prestige, selfishness and self serving rule the day. Selfishness seems easier than unselfishness, however, it has no reward. Sitting back and letting others do for us what we can do for ourselves is easier, but this is all so self serving and wicked. Living according to our desires rather than living according to God's statutes seems easier, but what does it benefit us? What is not easy is helping others who have difficulties, especially when we ourselves may be having difficulties. God's rules require you to take *His* stand in *all* matters. Living according to God's commands, rather than your own desires is not easy. It takes tremendous love for Him and a remarkable desire to do His will. God wills that you follow Him rather than living according to your desires. When God commands us, we must be obedient and demonstrate that we are His, and that we love Him. Living for Christ is not easy, initially, but it becomes easier and joyous the more you practice it, and there is an immanent and awesome benefit. The benefit is your great new eternal mansion built in His house, in Zion, or the New Jerusalem, or wherever God so desires, where peace and love abound forever, along with incomprehensible joy! Jesus said it would not be easy, but it will be worth it! Do you love Him enough to put your desires aside and perform His ways, always? Please say yes I do, yes I can, and yes I will!

"Lo! Men who surrender unto Allah, and women who surrender, and men who believe and women who believe, and men who obey and women who obey, and men who speak the truth and women who speak the truth, and men who persevere (in righteousness) and women who persevere, and men who are humble and women who are humble, and men who give alms and women who give alms, and men who fast and women who fast, and men who guard their modesty and women who guard (their modesty), and men who remember Allah much and women who remember—Allah hath prepared for them forgiveness and vast reward.

(Book of Remembering Allah, Chapter 244 (33 : 35)[29]

---

[29] Yahya, Mam Abu Zakariy and An-nawawi, Bin Sharaf, <u>Riyadh-Us-Saleheen</u>,. (no copyright date), pgs, 668, 669

"We are bound to thank God always for you, brethren, as it is meet, because that your faith groweth exceedingly, and the charity of every one of you all toward each other aboundeth; so that we ourselves glory in you in the churches of God for your patience and faith in all your persecutions and tribulations that ye endure: which is a manifest token of the Righteous Judgment of God, that ye may be counted worthy of the Kingdom of God, for which ye also suffer."

(2 Thessalonians 1: 3-5)

"But we are bound to give thanks always to God for you, brethren beloved of the Lord, because God hath from the beginning chosen you to salvation through Sanctification of the Spirit and belief of the truth: where unto He called you by our gospel, to the obtaining of the Glory of our Lord Jesus Christ. Therefore, brethren, stand fast, and hold the traditions which ye have been taught, whether by word or our epistle. Now our Lord Jesus Christ Himself, and God, even our Father Which hath loved us, and hath given everlasting consolation and good hope through grace, comfort your hearts, and stablish you in every good word and work."

(2 Thessalonians 2: 13-17)

Stretch our your hands to the poor according to your strength. Hide not your silver in the earth. Help the faithful man in affliction, and affliction will not find you in the time of your trouble. And every grievous and cruel yoke that come upon you bear all for the sake of the Lord, and thus you will find your reward in the day of judgment. It is good to go morning, midday, and evening into the Lord's dwelling (prayer/meditation), for the glory of your Creator. Because every breathing thing glorifies Him, and every creature visible and invisible returns Him praise.[30]

---

[30] Charles, R. H., The Book of the Secrets of Enoch, (2006), pg. 109

"God came from Teman, and the Holy One from mount Paran. Selah. His Glory covered the heavens, and the earth was full of His praise."

(Habakkuk 3: 3)

"Then I looked and heard the voice of many angels, numbering thousands upon thousands, and ten thousand times ten thousand. They encircled the throne and the living creatures and the elders. In a loud voice they sang: "Worthy is the Lamb, Who was slain, to receive power and wealth and wisdom and strength and honor and glory and praise!" Then I heard every creature in heaven and on earth and under the earth and on the sea, and all that is in them singing: "To Him Who sits on the throne and to The Lamb be praise and honor and glory and power, for ever and ever!" The four living creatures said, "Amen," and the elders fell down and worshipped."

(Revelation 5:11-14) (NIV)

KEEP YOUR HEAD TO THE SKY

" . . . Let the skies pour down righteousness . . ."
(Isaiah 45: 8)

Keeping your head to the sky involves being equipped with the Word of God, our manual on how to live, how to respond to life circumstances on this earth plane, and being Spiritually built up; receiving the Spiritual Anointing of God, and the gifts and fruits of the Holy Spirit that gives us spiritual power, to initiate proper and powerful responses to life circumstances; the gift of discernment, which informs of the who, when, why, what, where and how of prayer and intercession; and walking and talking with God in every aspect of our lives and in strict obedience. As one pastor put it, staying in the *Godmosphere!*

"Now ye see that this is the true faith of God; yea, ye see that God will support, and keep, and preserve us, so long as we are faithful unto Him, and unto our faith, and our religion; and never will the Lord suffer that we shall be destroyed except we should fall into transgression and deny our faith.
(Alma 44:4) (Book of Mormon)

Because there are so many distractions, jobs, television, children, social and church events, worry, unmet needs, etc., this often seems difficult to accomplish. When you walk and talk with God, you are aware that He is with you continuously, if you have established a personal relationship with Him. Even in the most difficult of circumstances, it is then that He carries you and comforts you. Some people think that in order to talk to God, you have to spend several hours in your prayer closet in a frenzy of begging and beseeching God for His mercy. God does delight in our spending as much time with Him as humanly possible, but He also wants to hear from us when we are not begging, and we often forget Him in our day to day existence—just loving Him and spending quality time with Him. Morning prayer, as soon as you open your eyes, is a wonderful way to reconnect with the Father after a nights sleep. This is the time for prayers of thanksgiving, thanking Him for waking you up in your right mind, thanking Him that all your limbs are operational, thanking Him that every cell, organ, neutron, proton, electron in your body is operating just as He designed it. Thanking Him also for family, for good friends, for spiritual partners, and inviting Him to walk and talk with you throughout the day. Thank Him also for the trials and tribulations in your life, as these jolt us into higher spiritual evolvement, if we approach them with the faith of an over comer. The way to end morning prayer is to ask God to be with us throughout the day and night, because whatever we encounter during the course of our day and night, He will have the perfect solution when we ask for His assistance.

> "Trust in the Lord with all thine heart; and lean not unto thine own understanding. In all thy ways acknowledge Him, and He shall direct thy paths."
> (Proverbs 3: 5, 6)

Evening prayer, before we retire for sleep, is an excellent time for thanking God for being with us throughout all the events of the day, for keeping us and our loved ones safe, and providing the solutions we needed throughout the day, and just basking in His glory, wonderfulness, warmth, and love.

Meditate on His loving kindness, and just meditate on how much you're thankful for Him in your life. This is the best and often uninterrupted time that you can spend just loving on the Father. Guess what!? He will love you back. It is the time for mutual, reciprocal Spiritual love. Just keep falling in love with the Father everyday, and watch that mutual love grow and blossom into something most glorious, wonderful, and joyful. Minute prayers all throughout the day and night, lets God know that He is always on our mind, and we realize that without Him we are nothing, and can do nothing in righteous perfection. For example, thanking Him when just missed having a collision on the road, thanking Him that you only sprained your ankle and didn't break your leg, thanking Him that your child only came home with a black eye from a fight, and not in a box! Thanking Him for the aroma of the flowers in your garden, thanking Him for the beautiful weather of that day, thanking Him for the moonlight that illuminates your bedroom, with just the right amount of light. We know that God is the Creator of all things, but we often forget to thank Him for His many, creations that He has made for our pleasure. Remember prayer is not one sided. We must always remember to listen for God's response and believe His answer is the best resolution. This is the prayer life of our personal and loving relationship with our Father.

"Confess your faults one to another, and pray one for another, that ye may be healed. The effectual fervent prayer of a righteous man availeth much."

(James 5: 16)

When we pray to the Father, for ourselves, and for others, we can be healed in mind, spirit, body, and soul. Prayer is nourishment in all these realms, and our Father hears us readily when we communicate with Him for the good of all. Prayer is also our "alone time" with the Father. A time for deliciously wrapping ourselves in His love. It has been said that it is only the love of a few that is holding this planet together. However, its also the prayers of a few that is holding this planet together, and we must increase the numbers of those few. Because of all the adversity in the world, we must approach intervention with the weapon of praying in the Spirit and with the full amour of God, which is:

- The belt of truth—honesty with God, others, and ourselves.

- The breastplate of righteousness—obedience in our daily walk with Him.

- The shield of faith—clinging to the truth of God's never changing word.

- The helmet of salvation—guarding your mind, where the real battle exists.

- The sword of the Spirit—the Rhema Word of God, which directs us in all things.

"Praying always with all prayer and supplication in the Spirit, and watching thereunto with all perseverance and supplication for all saints."
(Ephesians 6: 18)

Spiritual warfare is very real, and prayer has a very militant purpose, and that is to overcome the dominion of darkness, and bring about change, love, and light in people, in this very chaotic world. **Be militant for Jesus!!!** You can only win these vast, invisible wars with nothing less than the power of God backing you through prayer. Prayer does change circumstances, not only in our lives, but in the Spirit realm. Since we wrestle against principalities and powers of darkness, then prayer is designed to accomplish something there, as well as here. Things that take place in the Spiritual realm will manifest in the physical realm. This is what Spiritual warfare is all about. Since we are in a Spiritual battle, then we need Spiritual power through praying in the Spirit. Being without prayer increases one's spiritual vulnerability. Once a person has changed in the Spirit as a result of consistent heartfelt prayer, that change will manifest in the physical also.

> "And whatsoever ye shall ask in My Name, that will I do, that the Father may be glorified in the Son. If ye shall ask any thing in My name I will do it."
> (John 14:13, 14)

When we keep our head to the sky, we remember God's gifts and His promises. We are no longer earth bound with desires of earthly things. We are His children (those who obediently know and love Him), and He wants every good thing for us, Spiritually and physically (to meet our needs). Despite all the despair that we see around us, we know that our Father will take care of us. Some trials and tribulations are necessary for our spiritual growth and development. This is the time to hold on to our Father's promises and know that you know, His word does not return to Him void. When He says He will do something, He will; not necessarily in our timing, but always right on time! We cannot see what He sees, or know what He knows, but we must always trust that He knows what we need to survive on this earth plane, and what we need to evolve Spiritually so that we may soon return home to be with Him.

We should have the faith of the unnamed Shunammite woman in 2 Kings 4: 18-36, who sent for the prophet Elisha when her son died unexpectedly. The prophet sent his servant ahead during the journey to questioned her, "Is it well with thee, is it well with thy husband, is it well with thy child?" She replied very assured in the power of God, **"IT IS WELL!!"** For some, it would be inconceivable to know how she could say this, knowing that her child is dead. It was her faith in the power and promises of God, which assured her that it would be alright, it would be well; and the prophet was able to bring her child out of clutches of death. Our God is immeasurable, and all powerful! Watching the news and seeing the fulfillment of biblical prophecy should delight the spirit. In the flesh, it may seem frighteningly ominous to some, but it is only for a brief time. It is an indication that Jesus is coming very soon. God has given us messages in His Word to help us prevail, and keep our heads to the sky.

"Be strong and of a good courage, fear not, nor be afraid of them: for the Lord thy God, He it is that doth go with thee; He will not fail thee, nor forsake thee."

(Deuteronomy 31: 6)

"Be strong and let us fight bravely for our people and the Cities of our God. The Lord will do what is good in His sight."

(2 Samuel 10: 12) (NIV)

"Can a woman forget her suckling child, that she should not have compassion for the son of her womb? Yea, they may forget, yet will I not forget thee."

(Isaiah 49: 15)

You see!? Our Father will never leave nor forsake us. He will never fail or forget us. He has said so in His Word. Believe above all that He is faithful. We are the fruit of His Spirit. Just as ripe fruit smells sweet, our spirits emit a sweet fragrance to our Father when we are obedient, commune with Him, and love others with the love of Christ. Therefore, His fragrance must be most delicious and aromatic beyond anything we can comprehend. Imagine, if you can, being embraced by total Love and Light, Spirit to spirit, and the fragrance thereof, one with the Father, in Mount Zion, the New Jerusalem, or Paradise. The thought is totally mind boggling, and I imagine difficult for most to conceive. However, it will happen, because He promised, and He cannot lie!

"But ye are come unto Mount Sion, and unto the City of the Living God, the Heavenly Jerusalem, and to an innumerable company of angels, to the general assembly and Church of the Firstborn, which are written in heaven, and to God the Judge of all, and to the spirits of just men made perfect."

(Hebrews 13:22, 23)

"Finally, brethren, whatsoever things are true, whatsoever things are honest, whatsoever things are just, whatsoever things are pure, whatsoever things are lovely, whatsoever things are of good report; if there be any virtue, and if there be any praise think on these things. Those things, which ye have both learned, and received, and heard, and seen in me, do: and the God of peace shall be with you."

(Philippians 4: 8,9)

"And God hath set some in the church, first apostles, secondarily prophets, thirdly teachers, after that miracles, then gifts of healings, helps, governments, diversities of tongues. Are all apostles? are all prophets? are all teachers? are all workers of miracles? Have all the gifts of healing? do all speak with tongues? Do all interpret? But covet earnestly the best gifts: and yet shew I unto you a more excellent way."

(1 Corinthians 12:27-31)

So, be beautiful unto the Lord in all your thoughts, words, and deeds. Love Him, and no other. Worship only Him, and have no other gods (deities, money, cars, houses, fashion, titles, drugs, etc). Don't permit yourself to be seduced by "things" that are temporary. The eternal is eternal—forever, and freely given to those who are faithful to the end. The things of this world are temporary, earned by the sweat of your brow, or some evil means. How foolish would it be to surrender the eternal for the temporary? Guard your heart, mind, soul, and spirit always. Keep your head to the sky in all things seeking the wonderment, beauty, fragrance, and gifts of our Father. His love is eternal and worth the wait. Keep your head to the sky, focused on all His gifts worth more than anything this planet could produce. Stay Spiritually minded, forsaking the lust of the dust (things) of this physical plane.

There is no fire like greed, no crime like hatred, no sorrow like separation, no sickness like hunger of heart, and no joy like the joy of freedom.[31]

"Here I am! I stand at the door and knock. If anyone hears My voice and opens the door, I will come in and eat with him, and he with Me. To him who overcomes, I will give the right to sit with Me on My throne, just as I overcame and sat down with My Father on His throne."

(Revelation 3:20, 21) (NIV)

---

[31] www.sapphyr.net/buddhist/buddhist-quotes.com

ABUNDANT BLESSINGS

"Follow after charity, and desire spiritual gifts, but rather that ye may prophecy. for he that speaketh an unknown tongue speaketh not unto men, but unto God: for no man understandeth him; howbeit in the Spirit he speaketh mysteries. but he that prophesieth speaketh unto men to edification, and exhortation and comfort. He that speaketh in an unknown tongue edifieth himself; but he that prophesieth edifieth the church. I would that ye all spake with tongues, but rather that ye prophesied: for greater is he that prophesieth than he that speaketh with tongues, except he interpret, that the church may receive edifying."

(1 Corinthians 14: 1-4)

When people think of blessings from God, they tend to thing of material things—riches, promotion, success, money, fast cars and extravagant houses. These are the things of the world, and we have already been instructed to be in the world, but not of it. We need to cease our pursuit of material wealth, the ways of the world, and it's fake blessings, and return to the All in All, our Heavenly Father, and the Greatest Blessing of all, His Son Jesus Christ, Who is our Redeemer, and the Blessings of the Holy Spirit. Our Father is the greatest gift giver of all. No one can ever out give

Him. God is the only source of *true* blessings. **The enemy has many of us thinking that material possessions are the *only* blessings from God. They are not the true blessings! They are the fruit of our labors!** This lie comes straight from the pit of hell, and has misguided many of our brethren into so-called, "prosperity" ministries. First, *whose* prosperity? Certainly not the body of Christ! Observe these ministers, where they live, what they drive, what they wear, their jewelry and adornments, if they own a jet, where they travel, and for what purposes. Then look at their congregations, blindly believing that they will one day have what these pastors have. So sad, and so very wicked! Yet these "believers" continue to pour their meager earnings into the pockets of these so called pastors hoping for the same "miracle blessing." It's akin to playing the lottery! These being deceived have no understanding that the "blessings" their "pastors" are receiving, is definitely not always of, or from God. Who from then? The enemy, who is so thrilled that this pastor is keeping God's people fixated on things, rather than on God, so that they might *never* receive the ***TRUE*** blessings of God. For this, the enemy would keep a pastor with the illusion of great riches and prosperity. Would God bless us with things that rot, rust, dissipate, and offer no lasting reward? These things are foolishness to Him!

Knowing the grace, mercy, forgiveness, and unconditional love of our Father on a personal level *is* riches and blessings. He said He would supply all our needs, not all our wants. Don't get it twisted! Let us explore some of God's abundant blessings that neither rot, nor rust, nor decay, and are everlasting:

> "That He would grant you, according to the riches of His glory, to be strengthened with might by His Spirit in the inner man; that Christ may dwell in your hearts by faith; that ye, being rooted and grounded in love, may be able to comprehend with all saints what is the breadth, and length, and depth, and height; and to know the love of Christ, which passeth knowledge, that ye might be filled with all the fullness of God. Now unto Him that is able to do exceeding abundantly above all that we ask or think, according to the power that worketh in us."
>
> (Ephesians 3: 16-20)

Abundant Blessings

"O the depth of the riches both of the wisdom and knowledge of God! How unsearchable are His judgment, and His ways past finding out!"
(Romans 11:33)

"How that in a great trial of affliction the abundance of their joy and their deep poverty abounded unto the riches of their liberality."
(2 Corinthians 8:2)

"Whereof I am made a minister, according to the dispensation of God which is given to me for you, to fulfill the word of God; even the mystery which hath been hid from ages and from generations, but now is made manifest to His saints: To whom God would make known what is the riches of the glory of this mystery among the. Gentiles; which is Christ in you, the hope of glory.
(Colossian 1:25-27)

"That their hearts might be comforted, being knit together in love and unto all riches of the full assurance of understanding, to the acknowledgement of the mystery of God, and of the Father, and of Christ; in Whom are hid all the treasures of wisdom and knowledge."
(Colossians 2: 2,3)

"Blessed be the God and Father of our Lord Jesus Christ, Who hath blessed us with all spiritual blessings in Heavenly places in Christ."
(Ephesians 1:3)

"A faithful man shall abound with blessings; but he that maketh haste to be rich shall not be innocent."
(Proverbs 28: 20)

"For the Grace of God that bringeth salvation hath appeared to all men, teaching us that, denying ungodliness and worldly lusts, we should live soberly, righteously and Godly, in this present world; looking for that blessed hope, and the glorious appearing of the Great God and our Savior Jesus Christ; Who gave Himself for us, that He might redeem us from all iniquity, and purify unto Himself a peculiar people, zealous of good works."

(Titus 2: 11-14)

In Deuteronomy the 28ᵗʰ chapter, Father God does speak of material blessings as reward for our obedience and faithfulness, however, these are perks, earthly, temporary, and only for our pleasure (and survival), and above all, *to be shared,* **while on this planet.** These are not the Spiritual, eternal, everlasting blessings that He speaks of consistently throughout His Word. It was never intended that we should focus *only* on the material (perks), and definitely not above the Spiritual blessings.

When Father God blesses us with materials, it is meant to be a community blessing, not just for us alone. We become stewards of that blessing (that is not ours only) to be a blessing to others. This is where the problem lies, because world leaders, pastors and ministers demonstrate no knowledge of this concept, or are just not teaching it. Then the blessed ones becomes so puffed up and pompous in their riches and/or "righteousness" that they believe God blessed them only. They now sees themselves as more deserving than others, "holier" than others, and begin the grandiose entitlement, and God-less behaviors.

The atheistic, or God-less, civilization is a huge affair of sense gratification, and everyone is now mad after money to keep up an empty show. Everyone is seeking money because that is the medium of exchange for sense-gratificatory objects. To expect peace in such an atmosphere of gold-rush pandemonium is a utopian dream. As long as there is even a slight tinge of madness for sense gratification, peace will remain far, far away. The reason is that by nature everyone is an eternal servitor of the Supreme Lord, and therefore we cannot enjoy anything for our personal interest. We have to employ everything in transcendental service for the interest of the Lord. This alone can bring about the desired peace. A part of the body cannot make itself satisfied; it can only serve the whole body and derive satisfaction from that service. But now everyone is busy in self-interested business, and no one is prepared to serve the Lord. That is the basic cause of material existence. From the highest executive administrator down to the lowest sweeper in the street, everyone is working with the thought of unlawful accumulation of wealth. But to work merely for one's self-interest is unlawful and destructive. Even the cultivation of spiritual realization merely for one's self-interest is unlawful and destructive. As a result of all the unlawful money-making, there is no scarcity of money in the world. But there is a scarcity of peace. Since the whole of our human energy has been diverted to this money-making, the money-making capacity of the total population has certainly increased. But the result is that such an unrestricted and unlawful inflation of money has created a bad economy and has enabled us to manufacture huge, costly weapons that created a bad economy and has enabled us to manufacture huge, costly weapons that threaten to destroy the very result of such money-making. Instead of enjoying peace, the leaders of big money-making countries are now making big plans how they can save themselves from the modern destructive weapons, and yet a huge sum of money is being thrown into the sea for experiments with such dreadful weapons. Such experiments are being carried out not only at huge monetary costs, but also at the cost of many poor lives, thereby binding such nations to the laws of karma. That is the illusion of material nature. As a result of the impulse for sense gratification, money is earned by spoiled energy, and it is then spent for the destruction of the human race. The energy of the human race is thus spoiled by the law of nature because that energy is diverted from the service of the Lord, Who is actually the owner of all energies.[32]

God is no respecter of persons. When one is blessed, it is intended that the one shares the blessing with the community, actively seeking out the needs of others. Christ is the Head of the church, and we are the church body, therefore we are all family, interrelated and interconnected. You would never see family or a loved one do without, when you are able to share. So

---

[32] Bhaktivedanta, A. C. and Prabhupada, Swami, <u>The Journey of Self Discovery</u>, (1997), pg 205

it should be with our Spiritual family. It is the expectation of our Father, and as His children we need to be obedient. We must always take care of our brothers and sisters in need, when we are able to do so. When we seek diligently for the spiritual blessing, the material blessings will manifest without effort. However if we are not being a good steward over God's property, sharing with our brothers and sisters in need, He will rescind the stewardship, and the material blessings (perks), and Spiritual blessings will dissipate. We must seek His Spirit, His heart, and His fragrance, and live to be obedient, faithful stewards, performing our assignments, and loving others just as Jesus has demonstrated. Want to be like Jesus? This is how it is done!

Obeying His Word completely is what gives us the fullness of the fellowship with YaHuWah and YaHuWShA, His Son. Obedience is how we return His endless love He has given us. You have just learned the secrets of the universe! Oneness with YaHuWaH, and YaHuWShA is the Torah! [33]

This also, is where we need to seek and consult the Holy Spirit for guidance. Sometimes people are in need because of their own laziness, craftiness, or co-dependence. The Holy Spirit will not permit you, the steward of God's property, to be used or taken advantage of. He will always reveal who we really need to help. If the Spirit says no, then it is no! When He says yes, hop, skip, and jump to be of service!!!

Remember all that we do is to glorify God. Some of our brothers and sisters don't understand this concept. When they thank us, we must remind them that the gift is from God, and to God be the glory. Our actions, as vessels of the Lord, are meant only to demonstrate His grace, mercy, love, and care; and to use this opportunity to teach them about our Father. Be careful not to steal God's glory! **Remember He is Jehovah Jireh, the God who supplies all our needs, and the glory belongs to Him alone!**

> "For though I would desire to glory, I shall not be a fool; for
> I will say the truth: but now I forbear, least any man should

---

[33]   www.theignoredtorah.com/perspective/html

think of me above that which he seeth me to be, or that he heareth of me. And lest I should be exalted above measure through the abundance of the revelations, there was given to me a thorn in the flesh, the messenger of satan to buffet me lest I should be exalted above measure. For this thing I besought the Lord thrice, that it might depart from me. And He said unto me, My grace is sufficient for thee: for my strength is made perfect in weakness. Most gladly therefore will I rather glory in my infirmities, that the power of Christ may rest upon me. Therefore I take pleasure in infirmities, in reproaches, in necessities, in persecutions, in distresses for Christ's sake: for when I am weak, then am I strong. I am become a fool in glorying; ye have compelled me: for I ought to have been commended of you: for in nothing am I behind the very Chiefest Apostles, though I be nothing."

(2 Corinthians 12: 6-11)

While you're running about seeking material blessings, God is very clear about the fate of those who are not seeking and hearing Him. Neither is He impressed with rituals and ceremonies. He desires a very personal and reciprocal loving relationship with you, where He speaks, you listen, and obey; and you cast your cares and concerns on Him. When He says give to someone less fortunate, that is exactly what you're expected to do. If you obey with a sincerely loving heart, this is what releases favor and the abundance of God's blessings. God loves a cheerful giver!

"If ye will not hear, and if ye will not lay it to heart, to give glory unto My Name, saith the Lord of hosts, I will even send a curse upon you, and I will curse your blessings: yea, I have cursed them already, because ye do not lay it to heart. Behold, I will corrupt your seed, and spread dung upon your faces, even the dung of your solemn feasts; and one shall take you away with it."

(Malachi 3: 2,3)

Some church leaders think if they pay a one time bill for a member of the congregation, that they have blessed someone. Perhaps it did help, but often is not nearly enough, and the Spirit may have instructed them to do more. We often try to rationalize not doing more by saying that's not the Holy Spirit. Prime example, during a church service, I was instructed to give the pastor of a small storefront church two hundred dollars (after I had already paid my tithes!) My immediate mental response was, "The devil is a liar!" But the Holy Spirit continued to urge me to do this. I obeyed as instructed. The pastors wife fell into his arms and began to bawl when she saw the check made out to him. I don't know what the need was, and I don't need to know; but her heartfelt response was the confirmation that there was indeed a serious need; and it was without a doubt that it was the Holy Spirit who instructed me to give to them, in order to glorify the Father. When we are living righteous and upright, and behind the veil, the enemy cannot even talk to us. That being said, there is no reason to be second guessing the Holy Spirit.

Our Father is a God of love, mercy, and tenderness; we must seek His Spirit, His heart, and His fragrance, and live to demonstrate these parts of His nature towards our brothers and sisters in need. It is a part of our assignment, and is so much needed in these very dark days, when the planet is in a depression, spiritually, economically, ecologically, and the people—mentally. Make our Father proud of us for our obedient, faithful and honest stewardship, and love for others, that Jesus has demonstrated. Again, want to be like Jesus? This is how it is done! To be blessed, and continue to be blessed, we must always be a blessing to others, impart the sincere love of Christ, and be very happy to do so. Remember the lyrics of a popular spiritual children's song, "This little light of mine, I'm gonna let it shine." It's not a little light, it's a Grand Light. It is the Light of Christ. When people see you, they should see the Light, Compassion, and Love of Jesus.

> "Only the Lord had a delight in thy fathers to love them, and he chose their seed after them, even you above all people, as it is this day. Circumcise therefore the foreskin of your heart, and be no more stiff necked."
>
> (Deuteronomy 10: 15,16)

"If the whole body therefore be full of light, having no part
dark, the whole shall be full of light, as when the bright shining
of a candle doth give thee light."
(Luke 11:36)

"But the path of the just is as the shining light, that shineth
more and more unto the perfect day."
(Proverbs 4: 18)

Let us always be mindful of God's laws, commands, and statutes. Remember
His commands to be loving, merciful, and kind to our spiritual family on
the earth. Let us provide relief for those that are suffering, weep with those
that are weeping, and being in service to our brethren in any manner that
we are able to. We must especially pray with those who are in need of
prayer, and teach those who are seeking the Divine knowledge of God,
His character, His love, His Spirit, His fragrance; and above all, we must
be consistently obedient. These are but a few of the keys to obtaining
an abundance of His blessings. Always separate the frivolous things of
the earth (houses, cars, clothes, promotions, success—perks), these are
foolishness in the sight of God. Let us keep our minds and hearts fixed on
Him, His ways, His Divine purpose for our lives, and the largest blessing
of all—returning home to be with him always.

"Nevertheless we, according to His promise, look for new
heavens and a new earth, wherein dwelleth righteousness.
Wherefore, beloved, seeing that ye look for such things, be
diligent that ye may be found of Him in peace, without spot
and blameless."
(2 Peter 3: 13, 14)

Returning home to be with our Father forever is the ultimate blessing.
In comparison to this, see how trivial and insignificant worldly blessings

(perks) are! Who would trade eternity with our Father for a few temporal perks? **Never loose sight on what the real purpose of our being on this planet is—doing what ever He commands, learning the lessons we predestined to learn, and to get back to our Father and our *real* home.**

DELIGHTING
THE HEART OF GOD

"Delight thyself also in the Lord: and He shall give thee the
desires of thy heart."
(Psalms 37:4)

What an honor and a privilege to be chosen by the Almighty God, our Father. He truly loves us, because there is no way we can ever deserve, or can ever earn His love. Our every thought, our every word, and our every action should be performed with the purpose of delighting the heart of God. We were fearfully and wondrously made for His pleasure, and in His image. We should always strive to be like Him, and a delight unto Him, rather than engaging in disappointing, burdensome behavior that provokes Him to wrath. We love our Father so much, because He first loved us, even when we didn't deserve His love, and even when we didn't love ourselves. There is no better way to show our love than through our total and complete obedience, our total and complete surrender to His will and His way, helping our brothers and sisters in need, living at the center of His Will, and thus being a delight to His heart.

"Search me, O God, and know my heart: try me, and know my thoughts: and see if there be any wicked way in me, and lead me in the way everlasting."

(Psalms 139: 23, 23)

There is quite a bit of literature on us delighting in God. However, literature on how we can delight God's heart is much lacking. Perhaps it is because we don't know what is delightful to Him. We will never know what is delightful to Him unless we spend more time with Him. The revelation of what is delightful from me to God, and what is delightful from you to God, is quite different, and very personal for each individual. It must be sought spirit to Spirit. It is but another gift of the Holy Spirit! It is important to know what delights God's heart, because if He is delighted in us, we should be more than delighted! Ways in which we can delight God's heart using our finite minds includes first, obeying His commandments and statutes with a joyous desire to please Him. God loves us all the more when we walk and talk in His ways. God delights in our praise and worship of Him when done with sincerity of heart, especially without the song, dance, and music, and especially in our prayer closets, so as not to be seen of men. He is most delighted with our very personal prayers to Him, our personal love for Him, our personal praise of Him, and our personal worship of Him. Minute prayers and worship acknowledge that we are always aware of His presence in, with and around us; and that we are delighted to be in His presence and commune with Him always, and at all times.

"The sacrifice of the wicked is an abomination unto the Lord: but the prayer of the upright is His delight. The way of the wicked is an abomination unto the Lord: but He loveth him that followeth after righteousness."

(Proverbs 15: 8,)

"I delight to do Thy will, O my God: yea, Thy law is within my heart."

(Psalms 40: 8)

Delighting the heart of our Father, should not be at all arduous. It is a privilege and a pleasure and it releases joy unspeakable! To know that our Father is pleased with all that we say, do, and think, should delight our own hearts. To live to please Him, as we walk through this evil world, makes the journey that much easier, and safer—we are under His Divine protection, because we have become the apple of His eye. God is delighted when we walk upright and in truthfulness, we already know He hates a lie, and hates a liar even more. He is our most trusted confident. Our secrets are safe with Him.

"Enter into His gates with thanksgiving, and into his courts with praise: be thankful unto Him, and bless His Name. For the Lord is good; His mercy is everlasting; and His truth endureth to all generations."
(Psalms 100: 4, 5)

"He trusted on the Lord that He would deliver him: let Him deliver him, seeing He delighted in him."
(Psalms 22: 8)

"Thus saith the Lord, let not the wise man glory in his wisdom, neither let the mighty man glory in his might, let not the rich man glory in his riches; but let him the glorieth glory in this, that he understandeth and knoweth me, that I Am the Lord which exercise loving kindness, judgment, and righteousness, in the earth: for in these things I delight saith the Lord."
(Jeremiah 9: 23, 24)

When we give thanks to the Lord for all that He has given us, it lets Him know that we take nothing for granted, and are very appreciative of all things. Especially when we go outside of ourselves and thank Him for creation—the magnificent red rock of Sedona, or the awesome beauty of the mountains in Virginia, or the first snow fall on Christmas eve, or the vibrantly changing colors of the leaves in fall, or the splendor of a field of aromatic flowers, or the wonderful colors of the butterflies, or the song of chirping crickets in summer, that lull us to sleep. He has created all of this and more for our pleasure and delight, and we must show our gratitude for being able to enjoy such wondrous spectacles of nature. It probably really delights God's heart when we thank Him for the good in any circumstance of adversity. Thanking Him, for instance, for being demoted, instead of losing a job entirely, or thanking Him for the chicken on the table, when you're use to eating prime rib. Our Father is always blessing us, if we take the time to notice. It probably hurts God's heart when we miss the opportunity to thank Him for, what we may consider to be, the small and even insignificant things, because we always want what we can possess, and the biggest, the best, and brightest. Small, large, or nothing at all, there is always something to give God thanks and praise for. If we could but come out of ourselves, then we can see, hear, feel, taste, smell and appreciate the goodness, beauty, and fragrance, of our Father's Divine essence all around us.

Let us just appreciate and enjoy the majesty of all of creation. The beautiful lands filled with all types of beautiful vegetation, the crystal blue waters, the changing seasons with the array of colors that each brings, the multi colored and perfumed flowers of spring, the splendid changing colors of the leaves of fall, the stunning perennial growth of summer, the lightly dusted snow of winter, the white sands and blue waters of many beaches, the beauty of the mountains, animals, and fowl, just to name a few.

"I will praise Thee for ever, because Thou hast done it: and I will wait on Thy Name; for it is good before Thy saints."
(Psalms 52:9)

Delighting the Heart of God

JAH Thanks and Praises
(Jehovah Thanks and Praises)

Give thanks and praises unto JAH for everything His goodness send.
Give thanks and praises unto JAH for the shining sun for the moon and stars, for the food, clothing and the shelter.
Give thanks and praises unto JAH for everything His goodness sent.

Give thanks and praises unto JAH for the morning light, for rest and shelter of the night and for the blessings that fall from the clear blue sky.
Give thanks and praises unto JAH for His love and friend for his bountiful love will never end.

Give thanks and praises unto JAH for His righteous thought from His blessed heart; He will lead us apart in the part
that will make us pure and true
in the part He will show us what to do

Give thanks and praises unto JAH for His mercy and compassion upon I an I.
OH JAH OH JAH
I thank Thee for your love and friend and for everything your goodness send.
(Alanzo—Izo—Robinson)[34]

Jah!!! Rastafari!!! Ever living, ever true!

With all the confusion and disorder in the world today, it is a healthy diversion to take notice of all the beauty of the Father's creations. Step away from all the world's problems, your problems and issues, the problems and

---

[34] Anbesa, Judah, <u>Itations of Jamaica and I Rastafari</u>, (1987) pages unnumbered

issues of your family, community, and the world, to take minute vacations in the awesomeness of creation, and Divine Love. It was for man's pleasure that our Father created the splendor of His footstool, this earth. It is far better than any drug, or lasciviousness behavior. It is a delight to the spirit, and calming for the soul. This is but another way to spend time with, and give thanks and praise to our Father, for all that He has provided to us for our enjoyment. Remember God loved us so much that He provided awesome beauty, fragrance, and sensory pleasures all around us. We need to make the time to notice all the wonderful things our Father has given us for our pleasure. In the midst of all the madness, do take time to smell the flowers, and enjoy the song of the bluebird in early morning, and feel the warmth of the sun kissing your skin, and see the ethereal beauty all around you; and the Divinity within all things, that our Father has created for His pleasure and ours. This is quality time spent enjoying our Father's creation with Him. No doubt, this delights His heart, and yours as well. It assists us in realizing how mundane, temporary, and useless materials are; and the associated happiness temporary, as well. These concepts could not be better stated than in a poem written by Max Ehrmann in 1927:

Desiderata

Go placidly amid the noise and the haste, and remember what peace there may be in silence. As far as possible without surrender be on good terms with all persons. Speak you truth quietly and clearly; and listen to others, even to the dull and ignorant, they too have their story. Avoid loud and aggressive persons, they are vexations to the spirit.

If you compare yourself with others, you may become vain or bitter; for always there will be greater and lesser persons than yourself. Enjoy your achievements as well as your plans. Keep interested in your own career, however humble; it is a real possession in the changing fortunes of time.

Exercise caution in your business affairs, for the world is full of trickery. But let not this blind you to what virtue there is; many persons strive for high ideals, and everywhere life is full of heroism. Be yourself. Especially do not feign affection. Neither be cynical about love; for in the face of all aridity and disenchantment it is as perennial as the grass. Take kindly the counsel of the years, gracefully surrendering the things of youth.

Nurture strength of spirit to shield you in sudden misfortune. But do not distress yourself with dark imaginings. Many fears are born of fatigue and loneliness. Beyond a wholesome discipline, be gentle with yourself. You are a child of the universe, no less than the trees and the stars; you have a right to be here. And whether or not it is clear to you, no doubt the universe is unfolding as it should.

Therefore, be at peace with God, whatever you conceive Him to be. And whatever your labors and aspirations in the noisy confusion of life, keep peace in your soul. With all its sham, drudgery and broken dreams; it is still a beautiful world. Be cheerful.

Strive to be happy.[35]

---

[35] www/Marilee.us/desiderata.html

It seems Max Ehrmann placed some Biblical principles in this single poem. Living according to what our Father has specified in His Word, is the formula for having a peaceful existence on this earth plane, despite the commotion and confusion around us. Give audience to the Holy Spirit at all times. He will keep us calm and centered with whisperings of comfort, joy, and resolutions for our issues. When we are calm and joyous, we are then able to delight the heart of God in all our doings. We must remember, all this madness in the world around us, is a planned distraction to keep our focus on the world, and not on God. It is a deceitful trick of the enemy and *his* "children," who are *temporarily* running things on this planet. Do not fall prey to this, and do not be deceived by this. **Remember, God *is* still, and *will always be* in control. If our Father, the Master of the Universe, is in control, what need is there to worry about *anything*?** Delight His heart daily by exercising your faith in the fact that He loves you, will provide all your needs, and loves nothing more than spending quality time with you in prayer, meditation, and giving Him thanks, praise and glory!

"In my distress I called upon the Lord, and cried to my God: and He did hear my voice out of His temple, and my cry did enter into His ears. Then the earth shook and trembled; the foundations of heaven moved and shook, because He was wroth."

(2 Samuel 22: 7, 8)

"He delivered me from my strong enemy, and from them that hated me; for they were too strong for me. They prevented me in the day of my calamity: but the Lord was my stay. He brought me forth also into a large place: He delivered me, because He delighted in me. The Lord rewarded me according to my righteousness: according to the cleanness of my hands hath He recompensed me. For I have kept the ways of the Lord, and have not wickedly departed from my God."

(2 Samuel 22: 18-22)

"For such as be blessed of Him shall inherit the earth; and they that be cursed of Him shall be cut off. The steps of a good man are ordered by the Lord: and He delighteth in His way. Though he fall, he shall not be utterly cast down; for the Lord upholdeth Him with His hand."
(Psalms 37: 22-24)

"And all nations shall call you blessed; for ye shall be a delightsome land, saith the Lord of Hosts."
(Malachi 3: 12)

"The meek shall inherit the earth; and shall delight themselves in the abundance of peace."
(Psalms 37:11)

Which do you prefer, blessings or curses? Be delightful to the Lord in all your ways that He may bless you and your seed bountifully. How would you like to be the twinkle in God's eye, the star of His heavens and earth, the chuckle in His throat, the delight of His heart!? We must earnestly seek to be a joy to Him in all things. Connect your spirit to His Spirit by way of the Holy Spirit, and strive to be a delight to Him always. There can be no greater bliss! Perceive, to the extent that you can, with your finite mind; a very personal relationship with the Father. A Father, that you can tell all things. A Father Who will not reveal your inner most secrets. A Father that you can make laugh aloud, and Who will make you laugh also. A Father Who delights in your efforts to be just like His First Begotten Son, and Who will tell you so. A Father Who talks to you throughout the day, guiding, advising, and tickling your heart. A Father Who walks with you throughout the day, and keeps your walk among the faithful. A Father who is more than delighted when you help a stranger. A Father who is delighted when you unselfishly go the extra mile, in obedience, to perform whatever He has asked you to do. A Father who delights in your delight, to be in loving service to the least of His little ones. A Father Who loves you always because you have done all that He has commissioned you to do, and more, with a joyful and sincere heart. A Father Who rewards you for your obedience and service, with earthly perks, with greater Spiritual evolvement, and more importantly with rewards everlasting—eternal life with Him. This is the ultimate love relationship between Father and child. Go for it!!!

SOARING INTO ZION

"For God will save Zion, and will build the cities of Judah: that
they may dwell there, and have it in possession. The seed also
of His servants shall inherit it: and they that love His Name
shall dwell therein."

(Psalms 69: 35, 36)

In the Bible, Zion represents various things, though first and foremost,
it is the name of the Holy hill of Jerusalem, on one of the hills on
which the city was founded. (Psalm 81:1-3, "His foundation is in the
Holy Mountains. The Lord loveth the gates of Zion more than all the
dwellings of Jacob. Glorious things are spoken of thee, O City of God.
Selah"). Mount Zion became sacred when King David brought the Ark
of the Covenant to rest there. However, the name Zion was also used in
a wider sense to refer to the Temple of Jerusalem, or even to the whole of
Israel. Zion was the pride and heritage of Israel and the Holy dwelling
place of God (Psalm 9:11, "Sing praises to the Lord, which dwelleth in
Zion: declare among the people His doings." It is not difficult to imagine
therefore the great emotional significance Zion must have held for the
Jews (correction—Hebrews) who were exiled in Babylon after the fall of
Jerusalem (Psalm 137: 1-4, "By the rivers of Babylon, there we sat down,

yea, we wept, when we remembered Zion . . . How shall we sing the Lord's song in a strange land?")[36]

(Heavenly) Jerusalem is Zion, the Holy City of the Royal Divine King. Wherever God is—there is Zion and the Temple of His Presence, because God is, God of all the earth and (His) people, (Spiritual) Israel. Zion represents God, His Holiness, His Holy Presence, and His Holy people. (God has expectations and knowledge for His people.) : (1) Proclaim peace, proclaim salvation, say to Zion, "Your God reigns (Isaiah 62:11,12) "Behold, the Lord hath proclaimed unto the end of the world, say ye to the daughter of Zion, Behold, thy salvation cometh; behold, His reward is with Him, and His work before Him. And they shall call them, the Holy people, the redeemed of the Lord; and thou shalt be called, sought out, a city not forsaken." (2) Pray for fulfillment (of God's will). (3) The Spiritual restoration of Zion (Isaiah 4:3, "And it shall come to pass, that he that is left in Zion, and he that remaineth in Jerusalem, shall be called Holy, even every one that is written among the living in Jerusalem." (4) Jesus is the personification of Zion, (1 Peter 2: 6), "Wherefore also it is contained in the scripture, behold, I lay in Sion a Chief Corner Stone, elect, precious: and he that believeth on Him shall not be confounded."(5) It is from Zion that God's words go forth and His works are seen, (Micah 4: 2 "And many nations shall come, and say, come, and let us go up to the mountain of the Lord, and to the House of God of Jacob; and He will teach us of His ways, and we will walk in His paths: for the law shall go forth of Zion, and the Word of the Lord from Jerusalem."(6) Be blessed out of Zion, (Psalm 20: 2, "Send thee help from the sanctuary, and strengthen thee out of Zion.") (Psalm 128: 5 "The Lord shall bless thee out of Zion; and thou shalt see the good of Jerusalem all the days of thy life."). (Psalm 134: 3. "The Lord that made heaven and earth bless thee out of Zion." (7) We will be part of Zion, (Hebrews 1: 22 "But ye are come unto Mount Sion, and unto the City of the Living God, the Heavenly Jerusalem, and to an innumerable company of angels." [37]

---

36 www.homepage.ntlword.com

37 www.watchmanpost.com

"They that trust in the Lord shall be as Mount Zion, which cannot be removed, but abideth forever. As the mountains are round about Jerusalem, so the Lord is round about His people from henceforth even forever."

(Psalms 125: 1, 2)

"The righteous (will be) amid gardens and fountains (of clear-flowing water). (Their greeting will be); "Enter ye here in peace and security." And We shall remove from their hearts any lurking sense of injury: (They will be) brothers (joyfully) facing each other on thrones (of dignity). There no sense of fatigue shall touch them, nor shall they (ever) be asked to leave. Tell my servants that I am indeed the oft-forgiving, Most Merciful."

(Surah 15: 45-49)[38]

This is the beginning of the end of our journey on this planet. We have chosen to come to this earth plane, unawares, once we reached here. We have experienced both good and evil, and everything in between. We have learned the Spiritual lessons that we agreed to come here to learn, through pain, suffering, tears, and grief. We have evolved spiritually to the next level for some, and for others many levels, and are now yearning, and actively performing our assignments so that we may return home, to be with our Father.

"And I will give unto thee the keys of the Kingdom of Heaven: and whatsoever thou shalt bind on earth shall be bound in heaven: and whatsoever thou loose on earth shall be loosed in heaven."

(Matthew 16:19)

---

[38] Ali, Abdullah Yusuf, <u>The Meaning of the Holy Quaran</u>, (1991), pgs. 627, 628

Zion is our real home, *not* this earth realm. We are merely visitors on earth, to be tried and tested, to learn to recognize good and evil; to support one another with the love of Christ; so that we are able to fully appreciate the good when we return home. **We chose to come here, at this particular time, place, and circumstance, to enhance our Spiritual evolvement.** Remember our Father said He knew us before He placed us in our mother's wombs.

Since on this earth plane, the enemy has provided, and we have drank from the "waters of forgetfulness" that had placed us in a Spiritual stupor, so that we would forget who we really are, where we really came from, and the real and true purpose for coming here. However our Father God had a plan to help us remember. He sent His Rhema Word in human flesh, Divinity and humanity, to be able to experience all that we experience in the flesh on this earth plane, to judge us, and to save us. He taught us how to connect our spirit (Divine Spark), with the Spirit of our Father. He gave us His written word as a road map disclosing the paths we must take in order to return Home. We may have ignored the map, choosing to take another path, or not even looked at the map at all until now. **We that are *truly* His, will return to the true path and *will* find our way Home. The spark of Divinity that He placed in each one of us, is our link to Him, who we really are, why we came here, and how to get back home. Home is where you are loved.**

This earth plane does not love us, in fact it hates us; but our trip here was necessary so that we could grow into the deeper things of our Father, appreciate His indescribable love, bask in the fragrance of His joy, and revel in living life eternal with Him. Think about it. When we were with the Father prior to coming to this earth plane, all we knew was goodness. It would be very difficult to appreciate this goodness without having something to compare it to—experiencing the "badness." When we return home to our Father forever, our knowledge, our joy, our love, and our appreciation of Him will have its ultimate fulfillment. When we sit at the Feet of our Father, and Jesus we will not remember the difficulties of the earth with sorrow, but with all the things that will be revealed by our Father, the fulfillment of our joy will be too immensely wonderful for words!

"That the God of our Lord Jesus Christ, the Father of Glory, may give unto you the Spirit of Wisdom and Revelation in the knowledge of Him: The eyes of your understanding being enlightened; that ye may know what is the hope of His calling, and what the riches of the Glory of His inheritance in the saints, and what is the exceeding Greatness of His Power to us-ward who believe, according to the working of His Mighty Power, which He wrought in Christ, when He raised Him from the dead, and set Him at His Own Right Hand in the heavenly places, far above all principality, and power, and might, and dominion, and every name that is named, not only in this world, but also in that which is to come: and hath put all things under His feet, and gave Him to be the Head over all things to the church, which is His body, the fullness of Him that filleth all in all."

(Ephesians 2:17-23)

Try to imagine incomprehensible joy. We cannot. It is a misnomer. If it is incomprehensible, how can we imagine it with our finite minds? That is the very point! We can only perceive of the infinite, with an infinite mind! We cannot conceive of anything in our Father's house in the flesh. It is beyond, what we can think, know, or imagine. Just know that it is so ethereally beautiful and wondrous beyond anything we can imagine, or describe on this earth plane, and with this earth language. Our goal is to live in obedience, perform our Divine assignments in the army of the Lord, and return to our home in Zion to live with our Father forever.

Be still, my soul; the hour is hast'ning on
When we shall be forever with the Lord,
When disappointment, grief and fear are gone,
Sorrow forgot, love's purest joys restored.
Be still my soul; when change and tears are past
All safe and blessed we shall meet at last.[39]

Come, all ye Saints of Zion,
And let us praise the Lord;
His ransomed are returning,
According to His Word.
In sacred song and gladness
They walk the narrow way,
And thank the Lord
Who brought them
To see the latter day.[40]

Beautiful crowns on ev'ry brow
Beautiful palms the conq'rors show,
Beautiful robes the ransomed wear;
Beautiful all who enter there;
Thither I press with eager feet
Worshipping at the Savior's feet
There shall my rest be long and sweet
Zion, Zion, lovely Zion;
Beautiful Zion;
Zion, City of our God![41]

---

[39] Hymns of the Church of Jesus Christ of Latter Day Saints, (1998) # 124, 38, 44

[40] Hymns of the Church of Jesus Christ of Latter Day Saints, (1998) # 124, 38, 44

[41] Hymns of the Church of Jesus Christ of Latter Day Saints, (1998) # 124, 38, 44

"In my Father's house are many mansions: if it were not so, I would have told you. I go to prepare a place for you. And if I go and prepare a place for you, I will come again, and receive you unto Myself; that where I Am, there ye may be also."

(John 14: 2, 3)

> My Lord He calls me,
> He calls me by the thunder.
> The trumpet sounds within-a my soul,
> I ain't got long to stay here.[42]

"Behold I shew you a mystery; we shall not all sleep, but we shall all be changed, in a moment, in the twinkling of an eye, at the last trump; for all shall be raised incorruptible, and shall be changed. For this corruptible must put on incorruption, and this mortal must put on immortality. So when this corruptible shall have put on incorruption, and this mortal shall have put on immortality, then shall be brought to pass the saying that is written, death is swallowed up in victory."

(1 Corinthians 15: 51-53)

"And the ransomed of the Lord shall return, and come to Zion with songs and everlasting joy upon their heads: they shall obtain joy and gladness, and sorrow and sighing shall flee away."

(Isaiah 25: 10)

"Of His Kingdom there shall be no end."

(Luke 1:33)

And we will sing the Lord's song, in our own land!!!

---

[42] Jackson-Opoku, Sandra, The River Where Blood is Born, (1998), pg 104

BIBLIOGRAPHY

Ali, Abdullah Yusuf, The Meaning of the Holy Quaran, (1991), pgs. 627-628

Anbesa, Judah, Itations of Jamaica and I Rastafari, (1987), pages unnumbered

Anderson, Roy Allen, The Illuminati 666, (1983), pgs. 252, 253

Bailey, Patricia, Step into Divine Destiny, (2003), pgs. 49-53, and 212

Bhaktivedanta, A. C., and Prabhapada, Swami, The Journey of Self, (1997), pgs 9, 64, 205

Brown, Michael H., Prayer of the Warrior, (1993), pgs 1, 2, 111, 112

Charles, R. H., The Book of the Secrets of Enoch, (2006), pg. 109

Crouch, Paul, The Shadow of the Apocalypse, (1995), pgs. 49-56, 56-63

Duffield, Guy P. and Van Cleave, Nathaniel M., Foundations of Pentecostal Theology, (1987), pg. 2

Estulin, Daniel, The True Story of the Bilderberg Group, (2007), pg. 63

Hymns of the Church of Jesus Christ of Latter Day Saints, (1998), #'s 124, 38, 44

Jackson-Opoku, Sandra, The River Where Blood is Born, (1998), pg. 104

Martin, Walter, The Kingdom of the Occult, (1989), pg. 551

Neader, Agustus, History of the Christian Religion and Church During the Three First Centuries, translated from the German by H. J. Rose, (1848), pg. 16

Nibley, Hugh, Enoch The Prophet, (1986), pgs. 8-10, 178-180

Nickelsburg, George W. E. and Vanderkam, James C., 1 Enoch, (2004), pgs 148, 169

Prophet, Elizabeth Clare, Fallen Angels and Origins of Evil, (2000), pgs. 7, 8, 68

Readers Digest, Mysteries of the Bible, (1998), pg. 134

Talmage, James E., <u>Jesus The Christ</u>, pgs 746-749

Theo Quest.com, <u>The Quest for God is Everything</u>, (2002), pg. 5

Wilkerson, <u>David, God's Plan to Protect His People in the Coming Depression</u>, (1998), Pg. 2

www.askville.amgon.om/billionaires-world/AnswerView

www.bibleknowledge.com

www.homepage.ntlword.com

www.marilee.us/desiderata.html

www.sapphyr.net/buddhist/buddhist-quotes.com

www.theignoredtorah.com/perspectives/html

www.watchmanpost.com

Yahya, Mam Abu Zackariy, and An-nawawi, Bin Sharaf, <u>Riyadh-US-Saleheen</u> (no copyright date), pgs 668, 669